GOMERY'S BLINDERS AND

CANADIAN FEDERALISM

GOMERY'S BLINDERS AND
CANADIAN FEDERALISM

Ruth Hubbard
and
Gilles Paquet

University of
Ottawa Press

The University of Ottawa Press gratefully acknowledges the support extended to its publishing programme by the Canada Council for the Arts and the University of Ottawa.

We also acknowledge with gratitude the support of the Government of Canada through its Book Publishing Industry Development Program for our publishing activities.

Library and Archives Canada Cataloguing in Publication

Hubbard, Ruth, 1942-

    Gomery's blinders and Canadian federalism / Ruth Hubbard and Gilles Paquet.

Includes bibliographical references and index.
ISBN-13: 978-0-7766-0641-5
ISBN-10: 0-7766-0641-7

    1. Canada. Commission of Inquiry into the Sponsorship Program and Advertising Activities. 2. Sponsorship Scandal, Canada, 1997-. 3. Federal government--Canada. 4. Federal-provincial relations--Canada. 5. Canada-- Politics and government--1993-2006. I. Paquet, Gilles, 1936- II. Title.

JL86.P8H82 2007   352.7'480971   C2006-906886-0

 University of
Ottawa Press

Copy-editing: Dallas Harrison
Cover design: Kevin Matthews
Typesetting: Brad Horning
Proofreading: David Bernardi
Cover photograph by: James Norminton

Published by the University of Ottawa Press, 2007
542 King Edward Avenue, Ottawa, Ontario K1N 6N5
press@uottawa.ca / www.uopress.uottawa.ca

Typeset in Palatino Linotype 10/12
Printed and bound in Canada

CONTENTS

[T]hese efforts have failed because their creators were unable to break out of the cultural assumption of the inevitability of the bureaucratic mode of organization.

—Virginia H. Hine (1977)

blind·er
Pronunciation: 'blIn-d&r
Function: *noun*
1 : either of two flaps on a horse's bridle to keep it from seeing objects at its sides
2 *plural* : a limitation or obstruction to sight or discernment

—Merriam-Webster's
Online English Dictionary

INTRODUCTION

> A little neglect may breed great mischief ... for want of a
> nail the shoe was lost; for want of a shoe the horse was
> lost; and for want of a horse the rider was lost.
> — Benjamin Franklin (1758)

It began in such a small way, with a federal cabinet minister asking the Office of the Auditor General, in late winter 2002, to look into the circumstances surrounding three small Canadian government contracts given to a Montreal firm (Groupaction), between 1996 and 1999, for sponsorship activities in Quebec. These activities had blossomed in Quebec at the time following the narrow victory of the federalist forces in the 1995 referendum on Quebec secession. Sponsorship activities were to increase the visibility of the federal government in Quebec, thereby purporting to celebrate the benefits of federalism.

The 1995 referendum had been held as a result of a certain malaise among a plurality of Quebeckers about the existing institutional order and about the ways in which the federation was run. On the occasion of the referendum, a substantial number of Quebeckers had expressed dissatisfaction with an overcentralized federal system that did not allow Quebec to exercise the full range of public powers needed to ensure the maintenance and progress of Quebec as a distinct society.

The auditor general's report revealed serious administrative irregularities. As a result, in early 2004 when the report was tabled, the Martin government decided that matters were serious enough to require a public inquiry. The resulting inquiry by Justice John H. Gomery was given a broad mandate: "to investigate and report on questions raised, *directly and indirectly*" (Gomery 2006, 207; emphasis added), by the audit. One might reasonably have expected that this inquiry would not focus narrowly on possible administrative misappropriation of some federal funds for sponsoring publicity events but would also examine the sources of the unease that had forced the Canadian federal government to indulge in these kinds of social marketing activities. Those perceived inadequacies of the existing federal system were obviously questions raised indirectly but sharply by the sponsorship affair.

Justice Gomery chose not to deal with these broader issues. As a result, he neither shone any light on the brand of Canadian federalism that appears to have become increasingly unable to deal effectively with citizens' expectations nor helped Canadians to start down the path toward a fundamental transformation of the Canadian political system likely to tame the restiveness that now roils just below its surface.

The Gomery saga covers a two-year period (2004–2006) during which Justice Gomery conducted a kind of one-man-show investigation that was carried live on television and became as popular as *Canadian Idol* or *Star Mania* in certain parts of the country. The judge's mandate was to illuminate what had happened and to recommend how such mishaps might be avoided in the future. The inquiry resulted in the publication of two reports dealing with these separate issues — one in the fall of 2005 and the other in the winter of 2006.

This book is *not* a critical review or evaluation of these reports, although we comment critically on both. Rather, it is an attempt to put the whole affair into perspective.

SPONSORSHIP AS *REVELATEUR*

The shenanigans at the root of the inquiry seem to point to no more than a small number of individuals caught up in a Groucho Marxian episode involving false invoices and money laundering. But this is much too superficial a view. The sponsorship affair revealed a fundamental fault line in Canada's federal political stewardship. Like a thread in a fabric, it brought to light the tensions between an existing federal-level officialdom trying to maintain the kind of central control of the country that it has had for decades and an emerging new way of thinking about the governing apparatus, one that could be much more decentralized.

This aspect was missed by a popular press that chose to focus almost exclusively on the vulnerability of the federal bureaucratic system to financial corruption. In fact, the bureaucratic system proved to be quite honest at the senior working level and below, if quite disingenuous at the most senior level. It was mainly by going around that bureaucracy that the conspirators had been able to succeed and the illicit dealings had been allowed to grow. But one cannot absolve the most senior bureaucracy from seemingly having been complicit with the governing political apparatus in some instances.

The most senior level of the federal bureaucracy appears to have chosen (wittingly or not) to join forces with a government determined to perpetuate the traditional hierarchical order, to maintain its own party's grip on power, and to use the most crass and futile methods to do so. The higher bureaucracy, like so many politicians, was wilfully blind to anything that it did not want to see. Instead of working with the executive to invent new means to ease the way for a new and more effective decentralized institutional order, it became complicit in bolstering a centralized and hierarchical system of Canadian stewardship that was proving to be increasingly inadequate.

This indictment of both the political apparatchiks in power and a fragment of the highest echelon of the federal bureaucracy requires clarification, since it raises questions about a range of officials. One should not conclude from our statement that the highest level of bureaucracy is the fundamental culprit or even the most important one. The responsibility for maintaining or helping to maintain a hyper-centralized regime that endangered the fabric of the country has to be shared by many over the past thirty-five years. Any apportioning of blame among politicians, super-bureaucrats, and officials depends in the final analysis on citizens' expectations about the behaviour of the different officials, given their burden of office.

Citizens expect that super-bureaucrats, such as the auditor general, will act with great prudence, that the prime minister and ministers of the crown will be predominantly public spirited and altruistic, and that the clerk of the Privy Council and deputy ministers will not remain silent in the face of abuse of power by politicians but will be accountable for both their action and their inaction. These high expectations are not always met. To the extent that others have even higher expectations (that all politicians and bureaucrats should serve the public, not only passively in avoiding misbehaviour but also actively in ensuring that the most effective and efficient stewardship apparatus is in place, setting aside other loyalties), they are bound to be even more disappointed when officials do not work actively and creatively to construct an ever more effective institutional order (Lachmann 1971). We suggest that the sponsorship affair has revealed a tragic failure to provide enlightened leadership.

FROM BIG G TO SMALL g

Obviously, the institutional order is always a work in progress. It is continually changing as circumstances and guiding values evolve. But at any time, one may, for the sake of convenience, roughly identify the broad features of both what appears to be the old institutional order in place (and under stress) and the new order in the process of emerging.

In recent decades, the institutional order in place has been the centralized, hierarchical, and state-centric Westminster order that has allowed big-G government—mainly federal politicians and the most senior bureaucrats—to play a central role in governing the country. In this scheme, the federal apparatus is the dominant figure. The emerging order is the decentralized, horizontal, and distributed-power order that one might label small-g governance, which attempts to provide effective coordination of all the relevant stakeholders (private, public, and civic but also federal, provincial-territorial, and local governments), each of which has some of the power, resources, and information necessary for effective stewardship, to influence the governing of the country (Paquet 1999a, 1999b, 2005d).

These two institutional orders are clearly competing for the stewardship of the country, and the terrains where they clash are numerous. But the old order is losing ground. As technical change, economic growth, and socio-cultural diversity increase, the new circumstances create a need for a heightened capacity for speed, flexibility, and innovation in the ongoing process of differential adjustments to change, and the old order seems to be relatively ineffective at this new game, in which learning is essential. The new game needs new forms of integration and coordination that not only embody a whole new way of thinking but also require a much greater degree of effective decentralization so that private, public, and social front-line organizations are empowered to respond more effectively to the challenges of an increasingly turbulent environment *selon leur esprit*.

Widely distributed concerns have become the new drivers of learning: they are based on new forms of bottom-up alliances and partnerships, rooted to a much greater degree in *moral* rather than *legal* or *formal* contracts (Paquet 1992). The new dynamics—calling for more decentralization, more and broader participation, and more bottom-up governing—have challenged the old order and, predictably and understandably, provoked deep-rooted resistance and countermoves.

Such political contestation is part of any healthy democracy. But if one political party dominates the political scene for a long time, it runs the risk of confusing the "public interest" with its own, and, in a Westminster-type system, its uppermost professional public service can easily fall victim to an equally unhealthy presumption that "it knows best" and that "best" is aligned with the direction set by the dominantly elected government rather than the government in power.

The federal Liberal Party has had a controlling influence over the political scene for most of the past century—holding power (usually majority power) for sixty-five of the past eighty-five years and holding uninterrupted majority power for the past thirteen years (until the 2006 election). In these circumstances, it is not surprising that the strong and deep-rooted resistance to a drift in the institutional order has been the product of a mixture of genuine attachment to a particular ideology and of a somewhat arrogant belief that only the federal Liberal Party view can echo what is in the hearts of most Canadians.

Countermoves to the drift toward a new order have been engineered by officials of all sorts (politicians and bureaucrats). The first line of argument used is that the only alternative to centralization is chaos, which is widely regarded as unacceptable. When this argument fails, the officials' approach is to abandon any rational discussion and to doggedly assert that any initiative that tends to erode the centralized bastion should be opposed by any means because it will not serve the existing order well. The artillery used has ranged from the politics of denial (asserting that alternative ways are unworkable or a logical impossibility), to public opinion massaging in the media (pundits famously engrossed by the old paradigm, endlessly repeating the line that the concerns expressed by citizens are about imaginary problems or are unreasonable, that someone must be in charge, etc.), to unholy efforts by the federal Liberal Party (the most important representative of the old order) to engage in dirty tricks to remain in power.

The sponsorship affair can be seen as just such a dirty trick, albeit a naïve and somewhat futile one: the root causes of concern within the federation run too deep to be eliminated by sheer advertising. The Gomery inquiry probed the sordid details of some dirty tricks but chose not to look at the deeper causes and sources of the problem: the inadequacy of big-G stewardship, the dysfunctions of an existing centralized governing apparatus that risks tearing the fabric of the country apart, and the active collusion of centralizing groups trying to defend the decaying status quo. Through selective blindness and reprehensible inattention, Gomery missed an opportunity to help the Canadian governance system evolve (as citizens could legitimately expect commissions of inquiry to do).

THE STORYLINE

In the chapters that follow, we provide an anatomy of the "Gomery failure."

Chapter 1 sketches some basic facts of the sponsorship affair and points out the ways in which the initial reactions of the Office of the Auditor General (OAG) and the Prime Minister's Office (PMO) were over the top and failed to inform the Canadian citizen in an appropriate, serene, and effective way.

The Prime Minister's Office overreacted to the excessive hand-wringing of the OAG. *Administrative mishaps* were squarely put at the centre of the stage. Citizens were told that the whole federal public administration system was broken, and a commission of inquiry was created to investigate the questions raised by the OAG report and to recommend ways to make repairs in order to avoid any repetition of such mishaps in the future.

Both the OAG and the PMO seemed to be unwilling to put this particular episode in perspective, to take into account the forces that had led to the disaffection with centralized federalism, and to recognize that it was this unease that had caused the federal Liberal government of the day to use these dirty tricks. Consequently, they refused to see these activities as *political mishaps,* as efforts to oppose the emerging new governance regime.

As Chapter 2 hints, it soon became clear to dispassionate observers that there was much more at stake than the misspending of a few millions of taxpayers' dollars. Underpinning the discontent of Quebeckers (and the perceived need to persuade them otherwise) was (and remains) a questioning of the way in which Canadian federalism operates. The appropriate degree of true decentralization required for the Canadian federation to survive and to thrive was indeed (and remains) the elephant in the room, and much would depend on Gomery's willingness to recognize its existence.

Chapter 3 deals with Gomery's modus operandi as it transpired from witnessing the TV coverage. It examines the details of what took place through the lens of the actions of the deputy minister in charge of the department where the misappropriations occurred, as reported when he took the stand.

The Quail testimony demonstrates the challenges of managing the political/administrative interface in today's world of blurring boundaries and increased complexity. It shows the extent to which formal systems of accountability, which are rooted too rigidly in the Canadian version of the Westminster model, allowed key players (e.g., deputy ministers and the clerk of the Privy Council) to evade responsibility.

Chapter 4 deals explicitly with the first report of Justice Gomery and its determination to pronounce guilt and innocence in a world of distributed governance where such pronouncements are quite difficult and might not be appropriate. It shows that Gomery was led to mount a seriously flawed inquiry—thrust as he was into the overheated situation of a daily soap opera fraught with political gamesmanship, without clear rules of evidence to assist him in sifting conflicting testimony and with an insufficient understanding of the complex apparatus of government decision making.

Chapter 5 examines the repairs that are proposed in the second Gomery report and cautions (though somewhat belatedly, since the Gomery dynamics have already led to yet other overreactions) Prime Minister Harper's new government against accepting the Gomery recommendations holus-bolus. It argues that Justice Gomery's set of recommendations includes a few that are helpful (if banal) as well as some that are certainly unworkable in practice. But, most importantly, it argues that some are wrong-headed and downright dangerous if governance is to be effective.

Chapter 6 examines what Justice Gomery failed or refused to see. It fleshes out the features of the new public sector that is in the process of emerging and what it entails for public sector reform. Then it shows the inadequacy and inaccuracy of the Canadian model of public administration that is currently in good currency in official federal circles and taken as gospel by Gomery.

This analysis attempts to gauge the full measure of Gomery's failures that are ascribable not only to sloppy work but also and mostly to the refusal to take into account the broader context and the blind acceptance of many false assumptions. To use a Will Rogers turn of phrase, it is not so much what Justice Gomery did not know that was problematic—it was what he *thought* he knew that was not in fact so.

The conclusion suggests that although the Gomery Commission did not produce a *perestroika* ("restructuring") blueprint for transforming the federation, as some had hoped, it was not a complete failure. Unwittingly, and maybe as an unforeseen and unintended consequence, it provided a great deal of social learning and contributed to the January 23, 2006, election being a watershed—the first one in a long time to be fought over differing philosophies of federalism.

But we must quickly add that the nature of the public debate since then has not been fully conclusive. At times, the

Conservative government has been wavering in its support for a radical decentralization agenda. When combined with the reaffirmation of a robust centralization credo in the Liberal Party leadership debates (with appropriate sharps and flats), this suggests that the imperative choice between these two sharply different views of federalism may not yet be as front and centre as it should be. This choice may have to wait until the next election, but it might well not be the ballot question.

In closing, we propose a succinct set of lessons that may be drawn from this episode, a vignette of the sort of open-source Canadian federalism that may be in the making but also a set of conditions that may be regarded as prerequisites for the *perestroika* to materialize. Whether the Gomery saga as a useful source of long-term potential social learning can ever compensate for his less than adequate forensic inquiry in the short term is for the reader to decide.

We would like to thank colleagues at the Centre on Governance of the University of Ottawa and at INVENIRE for the many discussions in which many of these arguments have taken shape. We are also grateful for the comments made by the three reviewers of this manuscript: their comments were most useful and have led to a substantial improvement of the book. As will become obvious to them, we have not been able (or willing) to respond to all their criticisms to their full satisfaction, so they should not be regarded as guilty, by association, for our ruminations. Finally, we are thankful to Anne Burgess, Marie Clausén, and Dallas Harrison for their editorial assistance.

THE $100 MILLION MIRAGE

"Beware of the man who works hard to learn something, learns it, and finds himself no wiser than before," Bokonon tells us. "He is full of murderous resentment of people who are ignorant without having come by their ignorance the hard way."

—Kurt Vonnegut, Jr. (1963)

INTRODUCTION

In a democratic system, there is a need on occasion for super-professionals (judges, auditors, etc., who stand above the fray) to intervene. They are asked to cut the Gordian knot of problems that are not apparently resolvable by political deliberation or to provide *l'heure juste* on particularly complex and opaque issues. These super-professionals are not infallible, but they have moral legitimacy, and thus they bear a commensurate responsibility to act with the highest degree of circumspection and prudence—like Ceasar's wife.

Super-professionals must avoid the temptation to overplay their hands or to indulge in inflammatory rhetoric or theatrics. The precautionary principle has to inform everything that they do and say; otherwise, they are in danger of being a source of misinformation for the citizenry, and this incorrect information may have disastrous unintended consequences.

It may not only damage the very authority that their oracles are purported to have but also contribute to public cynicism and to a weakening of the democratic process. Any imprudent statement by a super-professional is akin to the printing of counterfeit money by the Bank of Canada.

CRITICAL THINKING REQUIRED

The report of the Office of the Auditor General on the federal government sponsorship program raises questions on this score. There have been significant irregularities in the management of the Sponsorship Program, and there has been, we are told, deceit, fraud, and criminal misappropriation. All of these activities must be punished, and the crown attorney must extract (and has been extracting) retribution from the guilty parties in the bureaucracy or in the Chrétien government or the Martin government, either for criminal acts or for dereliction of duty.

But irregularities should not be lightly confused with fraud, nor administrative expediency with crime. Moreover, super-professionals must be extremely careful not to allow their statements—based on limited findings—to be interpreted as casting shadows over a whole government, a whole political party, or the whole of the federal public service. Indeed, super-bureaucrats are expected to circumscribe and carefully map the different sorts of problems with which they are confronted and to interpret the events that they have to decode with a full appreciation of the context.

In a world where investigative journalism and critical thinking by the citizenry are robust and vibrant, any imprudent statement by a super-bureaucrat is quickly trimmed to size. Unfortunately, in our world, critical thinking is a scarce commodity: the citizenry receives its information in fifteen-second sound bites and batches of 800-word sanctimonious sermons of self-anointed commentators with a great *urgence de conclure*. Given the herd mentality, these countervailing forces do not seem to work well. Consequently, it is important for super-professionals to be extremely careful and for ordinary, alert citizens to scrutinize vigilantly all statements coming from them.

A few astute observers of the Ottawa scene, such as John A. Chenier of *Inside Ottawa* and Allan Gregg on CBC Television and in the *Globe and Mail* (February 13, 2004), did note that the report of the OAG on the Sponsorship Program was open to question. Chenier suggested that a better contextual appreciation might have led to a better report (*Inside Ottawa*, February 11, 2004). One might add that greater prudence in verbal statements by the auditor general herself might have deterred some of the misleading reporting.

NEED FOR NUANCES
AND REASONABLE ASSUMPTIONS

The 1995 referendum left the federalist forces painfully aware of their failure in communicating the benefits of centralized federalism to Quebeckers, and it revealed that another referendum might break up the country. But seemingly it did not persuade the federal Liberals that their notion of hyper-centralized federalism might no longer be suitable in Canada. This, as we will show in the rest of this book, may have been the crucial mistake. Instead of dealing with the structural flaws, there was a temptation to wallpaper over the cracks.

That being said, a crisis was apprehended, even though its sources may have been ill diagnosed, and this may explain the use of irregular procedures. In times of war, for example, the procurement process is guided less by adequate procedures than by effectiveness and security. Therefore, it might not be sensible to assume that fully open competitive bidding was the only appropriate way to allocate funds for federal promotion in the aftermath of the 1995 referendum or to assume that efforts to shield those activities from the scrutiny of those fighting for separation can only be interpreted as attempts to hide nefarious intent.

The further complaints about the lack of explicit discussion in Parliament, and the lack of a complete paper trail, appear to suggest a focus on process without an adequate appreciation of the substance of the issues at stake and the circumstances surrounding these activities. As Chenier (2004) has argued, urgently needed were firms that were "competent, discreet, knowledgeable and committed." It is also obvious that this kind of seduction program (once the decision was taken to embark upon it) could not be conducted from Macy's window.

Of equal concern is the arithmetic that appears to merrily blend both production fees and commissions into a single lump of $100 million, with the suggestion that the entire sum was a reprehensible misuse of funds. This calculation is at best misleading. If a local farmer receives only ten cents for an egg that a local grocery store sells for thirty cents, this does not mean that the difference of twenty cents (which does not end up in the farmer's pocket) is made up of indefensible and reprehensible "commissions." Some portion of this difference may be unwarranted, but a big chunk of it is made up of the genuine and useful activities of packaging, transport, et cetera. In the same way, to lump together the entire $100 million of the Sponsorship Program as unwarranted, or excessive, or the result of criminal activities does not suffice, no matter how bombastically stated.

There are undoubtedly individuals and groups who took advantage of the panic in Ottawa to extract unreasonable commissions for their activities. There was also undoubtedly invoice falsification and misuse of public funds, and these activities should be identified and should lead to indictment and prosecution. But to presume that all of the $100 million is made up of unwarranted and extortionate commissions is quite unwarranted and distortional.

The presumption that crown corporations had no business being involved in such sponsorship (and therefore no business being involved in joint ventures with the special unit doing the promotion campaign at Public Works) flies in the face of common sense. Canada Post, for example, probably has one-quarter of its business in Quebec. Action to salvage this market share by developing better visibility in Quebec (and taking advantage of the federal advertising spree to do so) seems to be defensible even if ultimately futile.

Finally, the complaint that the sponsorship programs were not spread evenly throughout the country (therefore reprehensible on this count as well) smacks of great naïveté. One deploys the activities of a program (like the police force or firefighting personnel) to the areas in danger—where there is a greater need for such activities.

However, the reader should not conclude from these critical comments of the report of the OAG that none of these activities was reprehensible. The sponsorship episode was certainly reprehensible at two levels. First, it was indeed revealed that there was fraudulent use of public funds by politicians and their friends. This abuse should be punished, and such federal "dirty tricks" should be prevented in the future by tighter rules—some financial repairs. Second, perhaps these efforts, naively meant to help regain citizens' trust in the federal system, missed the point. The source of disgruntlement about the federalism propounded by the federal Liberal Party (in Quebec but also in western Canada) may have less to do with lack of information and more to do with the autocratic philosophy of federalism in vogue in Ottawa. Indeed, the level of disgruntlement was such that some wanted to leave the federation. In this case, not only additional financial controls but also "philosophical repairs" might be required.

THE FEAR OF DENIAL

Equally surprising and reprehensible was Paul Martin's lack of critical reaction to the report of the OAG. So intense was his desire to distance himself from this electorally dangerous legacy of the previous government that Martin stood ready to lend credence to any claimed misdeeds, and to denounce them in a somewhat cavalier manner, as long as it was recognized that his own government had nothing to do with them. Instead of insisting that the real concerns might have been exaggerated, that one should clearly focus on the substantially smaller number of activities that were indeed reprehensible or criminal, or even that a flawed centralization philosophy might be the root cause of the problem, Martin and a horde of parliamentarians took refuge behind the virtuous screen of outrage and swallowed the $100 million mirage whole.

The citizenry certainly needed to know some specifics:

- whether the fees and commissions collected were out of line with the standards in the industry (because brokering deals often leaves the broker with liabilities that must be reasonably compensated); and
- whether there was outright fraud and to what extent this fraud was 1 percent, 5 percent, or 89 percent of the $100 million notional sum that has been batted about.

The $100 million metaphor, plus the infamous statement by the auditor general that "all the rules in the book have been broken," may make good headlines, but they also appear to be excessive statements at a time when considerable prudence was required. Not demanding that these statements from the OAG be tempered (and that the extent of the real misappropriations be fully documented) revealed a lack of *fortitudo* (a capacity to take into account the context and the longer time horizon) by parliamentarians, the press, and other stakeholders—who have shown themselves to be more interested in making political hay and in increased political ratings than in making the truth known. The OAG's lack of *temperentia* (a sense of limits, of not going too far) was unfortunate, but lack of *fortitudo* among parliamentarians and the press was equally damaging.

THE COSTS OF INACTION

The OAG is no more infallible or clairvoyant than the Supreme Court of Canada. And while both institutions do a good job most of the time, there is no reason to believe that, as with any human institution, they cannot err from time to time. Taking their utterances as gospel truth is dangerous, which is why, for instance, we have the "notwithstanding clause" to contain the Supreme Court's power. It is the responsibility of elected officials in a democracy to correct any unintended misstatement that the super-bureaucrats may make. Not to do so may be dangerous.

The first victim of such a failure of *temperantia* and *fortitudo* is democracy. The citizenry, bamboozled by half-truths, incomplete statements, and fits of theatrics, and poorly enlightened by a press that has indulged in a good deal of smart-alecky reporting in lieu of analysis, has become even more cynical. It has been incited not only to vent its anger at anything that might serve as a lightning rod — government, the Liberal Party, bureaucrats, et cetera — but also to do so blindly, ignorantly, and self-righteously. This is a step backward in the development of our democratic ethos.

The second victim is the state, which was unfairly tarnished by friends and foes as having become a broken system. It will find it much more difficult to play its proper role in the future, and this difficulty may be costly, for the state — while perhaps not as important as it once was — remains of central importance in a democracy. It is difficult to gauge the undue damage also done to the credibility and professionalism of the Canadian public service by these errors of judgment.

The third victim is the citizen, who can legitimately complain that she has been badly served by the super-bureaucrats, the parliamentarians, and the press. For the price that she pays, a citizen in our democratic system can reasonably expect that all sources of information will not fail at the same time. The citizenry has been betrayed. This betrayal may well translate into a lower turnout at the polls and a desertion of the political process.

THE FABRIC OF SOCIETY

Decisions made by people who share assumptions, even though there is no discussion between them, will produce actions so similar that there appears to be collusion even though the actors themselves feel they occupy conflicting positions.

—Virginia H. Hine (1977)

INTRODUCTION

The governing of modern democracies has evolved significantly over the past three or four decades. The traditional big-G centralized institutional order—top down, state centric, autocratic, hierarchical, bent on imposing sets of rules—has slowly been eroded (much like the power of the nation-state) by various leakages of legitimate authority: upward to international and world organizations such as the WTO, sideways to multinational firms or other private or social organizations such as Greenpeace and the like, and downward to regional and local organizations (private, public, and civic) that are often much better equipped to engineer effective reactions to the challenges of the transnational turbulent environment.

While nation-states could claim to be able to ensure security zones for their nationals in the past, this is now quasi-impossible. The competition from organizations from all over the world is putting pressure on all national concerns. Big-G government is now unable to ensure either the protection of nationals or the steering of the socio-economy according to their wishes for lack of the necessary levers to do so. In this new turbulent world, nobody seems to be in charge (Cleveland 2002).

Small-g governance has become the emerging mode of governing: it aims at ensuring effective coordination when power, resources, and information are widely distributed. In this new world of small-g governance, governing is more collaborative, horizontal, and democratic. It is less state centric, and government acquires a new set of roles: animateur rather than simply the monopolist of public coercion and regulation.

This new institutional order transforms the role of the state: the roles of the super-bureaucrats (e.g., the Office of the Auditor General and the Supreme Court), of the politicians (Parliament and the executive—the government of the day), and of the professional public service (in particular its uppermost level of deputy ministers, led by the clerk and other senior-level bureaucrats) have to be modified accordingly. They all have to become immensely less autocratic and much more attentive to the dangers of a culture of adjudication that may stifle innovation and productivity (Paquet 2006c). At the same time, and even more importantly, it also changes the role of the governed. If no one is in charge, citizens and communities must become involved and become producers of governance. Indeed, the governed can dissent, complain, and have more of an impact on decision making. This is a new responsibility for citizens, who are granted rights so that they can dispatch their roles responsibly and effectively.

The world of small-g governance is still *en émergence*. Big-G government will not vanish: it will continue to thrive in a variety of sectors (e.g., security, tax collection, etc.). In most domains, though, small-g governance will entail a much higher degree of consultation and negotiation with citizens than in previous eras. Indeed, the very range of relevant stakeholders to be consulted has already dramatically increased.

FEATURES OF THE EMERGING ORDER

This drift has transformed the nature of the socio-cultural system. It is generating a new division of labour among the private, public, and social sectors and among levels of government. It has also made the socio-technical system more vulnerable to hijacking by minorities of all sorts and has transformed the very notion of accountability and ethics.

First, the G-to-g drift has challenged both the state-centric and the centralized mindset that has dominated the Canadian scene for the past fifty years. This challenge has led both to a defensive stance by the central government and to an equally important defensive reaction by the state as a whole. Federal-provincial competition has become fiercer, and all governments have felt the pressure of having to develop new forms of relationships with the private and social sectors. On neither front has this new experience been without important challenges. These new relationships cannot be forged without much opposition and great difficulties.

Second, the attenuation of top-down coercion has left the system more vulnerable to the pressures of single-issue interest groups and other minorities who have tried to make the highest and best use of the remnants of central control by invoking all sorts of rationales (particularly human rights) to demand that their particular wishes be fulfilled. Indeed, groups have used the language of rights to redefine their preferences and wishes as entitlements. In many cases, minorities have been able to "make law." The relative power vacuum left by a weakened central government has not been left unfilled: super-bureaucrats in an activist Supreme Court or uppermost officials have seen opportunities for *collibration* (putting a thumb on the scale to tip it in what they regard as a desirable direction).

Third, when nobody is in charge, the very notions of accountability and ethics are transformed. The burden of office gets defined by a variety of stakeholders who have different and often contradictory expectations. The burden of office becomes naturally fuzzier. The fuzzier it becomes, the less clear what may be considered as expected and acceptable behaviour is—and therefore what one will have to be accountable for or what is ethically enforceable. One is condemned in this sort of world to ill-defined and/or soft accountabilities and fuzzy ethics.

As a result, scandals become much more difficult to adjudicate and disentangle. How is one to determine blame and what has to be done to effect the necessary repairs to the existing social architecture in the face of such complex circumstances? In the old autocratic order, mishaps had to be attributed to a guilty party, punishment had to be exacted, and rules had to be tightened if and when violations were noted; in the new collaborative order, mishaps often cannot be attributed to anyone in particular, guilt cannot be unequivocally determined on an individual basis, and tighter rules may be counterproductive. In the old order, more coercion was seen as a way to end unruly behaviour; in the new order, more freedom, more trust, and broader design repairs to the institutional order may represent a much more promising option.

THE DYNAMIC CONSERVATISM
OF THE OLD ORDER

As we mentioned earlier, the old order is quite resilient, and this resilience does not have a single source. It has roots in blockages and resistances at many levels: politicians, super-bureaucrats, and highest-order bureaucrats.

Pierre Elliott Trudeau was one of the most significant architects of the rear-guard action in defence of the old order at the time when it first came under attack. He resisted the request for more decentralization to such an extent, and he did it in such a spiteful way, that one may squarely ascribe to him the wrecking of any possibility of a smooth transition from the old order to the new.

Gordon Robertson, a former clerk of the Privy Council who worked closely with Mackenzie King, Louis St. Laurent, Lester Pearson, and Trudeau, has written that "Trudeau was philosophically and temperamentally less suited than Pearson—or King or St. Laurent—to the federal system of government with its constant need for agreement and compromise. He wanted decision, clarity, and a strong federal government" (2001, 378). Having "lost his faith in democracy" after nearly losing the 1972 election (Bliss 2004, 259), Trudeau adopted a most autocratic style and sowed the seeds of discontent both in Quebec and in western Canada. The country would reap the negative consequences of such intemperate actions for decades. Even after leaving office, Trudeau continued to fight fiercely, and often it seemed vindictively, and to sabotage efforts (e.g., the 1990 Meech Lake and the 1992 Charlottetown Accords) that would have eased in the new order smoothly. He did this in a manner that Robertson does not hesitate to call "unreasonable" and "destructive in intent" (2001, 339).

The super-bureaucrats were also a source of blockage. The newly activist Supreme Court in the wake of the Charter of Rights and Freedoms in 1982, and the expansion of the mandate of the Office of the Auditor General to deal with "value for money" audits (with no formal accountability link back to Parliament), provided these institutions with increased powers to interfere actively in the realm of the executive and the legislative branches of governments. They often used these powers to bolster the old order.

Finally, the independent but subordinate powers of the mandarins may have seemed to fade significantly (as the emphasis shifted from a world where the clerk and his or her close associates were working as partners with government leaders to one where they toiled more as mere fixers for their political masters). This fading has not meant, though, that all their capacity to interfere has vanished (Hubbard and Paquet 2006a).

For many decades, until the 1970s, when Canada faced significant challenges that demanded new and reshaped institutions and organizations, the uppermost levels of the bureaucracy worked as non-partisan partners of governments. During that long period, these mandarins were always conscious of their responsibility to pay great attention to the fabric of Canadian society. Speaking truth to power meant being willing to resign rather than betray this public trust. This notion began to change with the Trudeau era. In fact, Robertson reports that Trudeau's explanation for not choosing him (his former clerk) to return to his position as secretary to cabinet for federal-provincial relations after Clark's 1979 defeat was that he was "a mandarin, concerned with the common weal, afraid of irreparable damage to the fabric of society" (2001, 321).

Over recent decades, standing up against approaches that ran a high risk of doing irreparable damage to the fabric of Canadian society has acquired a quixotic label. Significant numbers of deputy ministers have resigned or have taken tough stands over the past few decades, of course, but the reasons and the principles that underpinned their decisions were either forgotten or disparaged as outdated within the corridors of power and, in any case, never mentioned outside the inner circles of the bureaucracy. The corridor of acceptable moral behaviour has been altered slowly but noticeably.

A MANICHEAN GOSPEL

One of the main fixtures of the reaction by politicians and senior officials to this institutional drift has been the gospel of firewalls: the pretense that one "may establish and sustain multiple institutions committed to different values, walling off each institution from the responsibilities of the others"

(Thacher and Rein 2004, 463). This view was propounded with much verve in the 1990s by Jane Jacobs (1992) and embraced warmly by the federal establishment, which has made it into an article of faith. For Jacobs, two orders cannot mix: *métissage* is the recipe for disaster. She has expounded her views using two orders (which one might reasonably call "state centric" and "liberal" but which she has baptized the "guardian" and the "commercial" syndromes). She has then argued that these two orders cannot mix without producing "monstrous hybrids."

This approach has been used both to fence off the state-centric apparatus from criticism (i.e., the role of the state as "guardian" is a sacred cow) and to bolster the centralized version of the state-centric apparatus as the only one that can ensure the requisite degree of redistribution called for by the guardian role. The ideas of partnership among sectors and of a blurring of institutions (what we have called *métissage*; Hubbard and Paquet 2002) are regarded as unacceptable and have come to underpin the bizarre view that any tinkering with the state, or any reduction of the size of the state, can only amount to an impoverishment of governance. This argument amounts, for all practical purposes, to an absolute defence of the old order of big-G government. It is hardly surprising that such a view has been wholeheartedly supported by many officials in Ottawa. They have found an intellectual defence of their preferred position in this philosophy.

The argument used to defend the sanctity of the guardian-trader frontier has also been put to use defending the other sacred cow: the inviolable boundary between politics and administration. Defenders of the Westminster model have argued that those two worlds cannot mix: the authority of the elected officials and Parliament over the hired bureaucrats has been presented as a one-way street where public administration is the humble servant of elected officials.

Our disagreement with the firewalls approach in both cases is based on two grounds. First, the new *métissage* at the interfaces not only of traders and guardians but also of politicians and bureaucrats need not produce "monstrous hybrids" but may indeed bring forth a superior arrangement, if only stakeholders can agree on a minimal covenant that will guide the construction of the new order. In other words, one need not be Manichean, for one may get the best of both worlds. Second, the Manichean/firewalls approach is tremendously destructive in that it not only prevents exploration of the whole range of institutional arrangements bound to emerge over time at these interfaces but also forces the debate into a stark either/or choice between the old order and the new order. It occludes the fact that mixed organizations exist and thrive, and it prevents the experimental construction of a new order *par morceaux* and *par étapes*.

CONCLUSION

The resilience of the old order is considerable, and the resistance to its fading—especially by those who owe it their power and status—is fierce. It will not give way quickly or cleanly but gradually and in bits and pieces. The extent to which Canadians are willing to adjust their postwar thinking about personal responsibility and entitlements remains to be seen.

Gomery as *glasnost* ("yearning for transparency") set the stage for Gomery as *perestroika* ("yearning for restructuring"). But there were roadblocks on that path. The strong tendencies toward de-responsibilization have not entirely vanished (and therefore the taste for centralization is strong), the neurosis has not been extinguished, and the federal apparatus still has a rather vibrant capacity for deception (the 1970s Trudeau chestnut line about the federal government not being reduced to the role of "headwaiter of the provinces" was resuscitated by Ignatieff in the fall of 2006) (Reynolds 2006). So it is not clear which choices Canadians will make if and when they are confronted with the fundamental choice between centralization (Liberal and NDP) and decentralization (Conservatives and Bloc).

THE QUAIL ENIGMA

Il se peut bien, dit Castor, que les principes qui règlent
l'administration des finances publiques soient un peu
trop métaphysiques.

— Alain (1934)

INTRODUCTION

The inquiry led by Justice John Gomery into the sponsorship
affair kept many people riveted to their television screens.
It pertained to a relatively small amount of taxpayers'
money (less than seven-tenths of 1 percent of the $19–$20
billion annual budget of the responsible department, Public
Works and Government Services Canada (PWGSC). But the
testimonies that emerged — envelopes stuffed with cash left on
restaurant tables, bills paid without much evidence of work
done, and the possibility that taxpayers' money was used to
fund a political party — generated much national ire.

One may reasonably ask, what went wrong? And what
could have been done to prevent such a fiasco? Our approach
to these questions focuses on one crucial official position: that
of the deputy minister who sits on the bureaucratic/political
boundary. Was this a simple case of failed oversight by a
deputy minister?

THE QUAIL ENIGMA

THE BURDEN OF OFFICE

Deputy ministers are expected to be competent, non-partisan, but politically sensitive; to be courageous enough to speak truth to power about the management requirements of government as well as about possible problems with policy or program ideas, including the risk of irreparable damage to the fabric of Canadian society; and to balance formal accountabilities to a minister, to the prime minister, to the Treasury Board, to the Public Service Commission, and in some cases to specific commitments (Kroeger 1996; Osbaldeston 1988).

This position requires considerable competence, experience, skill, and above all good judgment. Deputy ministers must loyally serve the government of the day while safeguarding the public trust (i.e., ensuring prudence and probity) and being loyal to the public good (i.e., putting it before their own personal interests). By design in Canada's Westminster system, and because they sit on the boundary between the political and the bureaucratic worlds, they play an especially important role.

There are no rules to guide their daily actions and decisions. The job is a craft that is usually carefully learned by doing and by watching role models over a relatively long period of time. And it carries a high risk. Appointed by order in council, on the recommendation of the prime minister of the day, deputy ministers virtually all serve at pleasure and thus can be moved, demoted, or fired at a moment's notice.

In these circumstances, beyond what they have learned along the way, their triangulation of context, organizational culture (allowing more or less latitude and initiative), and basic values provides guideposts. These three dimensions shape their behaviour and play an important role in determining the moral corridor for their work: the judgments that they make and the way in which these judgments translate into daily actions and decisions.

QUAIL'S CIRCUMSTANCES

It is against this backdrop, then, that we review the Quail enigma as displayed both by the role of Ran Quail (the PWGSC deputy minister from 1993 to April 2001) and by his testimony to Gomery and that of other key players. PWGSC was the agency overseeing the operations of those involved in the sponsorship affair (including advertising and later the sponsorship proposals that became the Sponsorship Program in November 1997).

Quail reported that he was aware that one of his subordinates, J. C. (Chuck) Guité, was handling the sponsorship file directly with personnel in the minister's office and the Prime Minister's Office, that he did not probe the matter with special attention (until early 2000, when he called for an internal audit), and that he did not report any unease about the unusual reporting relationship to the clerk of the Privy Council, although he ensured that the Privy Council Office was aware of it.

To be fair, Quail had inherited a file—public advertising—that had long been an albatross. Advertising contracts awarded by the federal government have traditionally been fraught with political/bureaucratic messiness. A desire to exercise central (and political) control has led in recent times to the development of a "prequalified" list of suppliers assigned to specific departments/agencies for one to four or more years, with specific arrangements negotiated by them according to need and with PWGSC providing the contracting.

The Chrétien government campaigned on a platform of greater transparency and competitiveness in this kind of contracting and gave instructions shortly after its election in 1993 for new contracting guidelines to be developed. In the area of advertising, the need was to balance greater transparency, openness to all qualified suppliers, and competitiveness with the political flexibility considered necessary.

In the case of advertising, the responsibility rested with departments for their own advertising campaigns, with the actual contracting carried out by PWGSC in accordance with the guidelines. In the case of sponsorship proposals, the entire accountability rested with PWGSC. The PWGSC manager responsible, Guité, admitted that he did not follow the guidelines that had been issued, either for advertising or for sponsorship proposals, because they were unworkable (Gomery 2004, 5730). And he reported that he did not advise his departmental superiors, the minister responsible, or the PMO of this view (Gomery 2004, 5725).

For his part, Quail concurred that he saw the sponsorship process as partitioned in three: (1) event selection and (2) amounts allotted (both being political decisions), followed by (3) the contractual arrangements for them (this last being carried out by PWGSC administration), with written assurances given to PWGSC's senior financial officer that once suppliers were chosen and the standing offer was in place, costs would be reasonable and in keeping with industry standards. One may reasonably ask, then, whether the deputy minister failed to exercise due diligence in the sponsorship file and why his involvement and behaviour received so little attention, despite his being such a central figure.

QUAIL'S ACTIONS
On the issue of due diligence, Quail noted that he assumed that the three stages of the new process were working well, in part because the necessary Treasury Board submissions during the period included assertions that the appropriate Treasury Board rules were being observed. An observer might conclude that he may have been less well informed than he should have been about how it was handled and managed during the entire period that Guité was in charge of things.

It is true that when, in the post-Guité era, Quail was made aware of irregularities he called for an internal audit and acted on the results immediately (PWGSC 2000). More broadly, once the reality of the non-compliance and problems came to light, actions were taken by the government to investigate the matter and to address the shortcomings. Covering the period from 2000 to June 2003, these measures included strengthening and modernizing management at a government-wide level, acting on sponsorship issues, and taking steps to strengthen advertising and public opinion research (GOC 2003b).

As to why Quail's behaviour did not receive much attention at the Gomery inquiry, that may be attributed to new arrangements that more specifically set out the duties of deputy ministers, and new guidelines had been issued in the meantime with the government's introduction of three initiatives: Guidance for Deputy Ministers, the Management Accountability Framework (MAF), and the Values and Ethics Code for the Public Service. In other words, things managerial could have been said to be largely resolved or "in hand."

This argument is not completely persuasive. By all accounts, the strategic vagueness of these directives entailed little effective guidance. In the aftermath of the Gomery revelations, actions were taken up and down the line in government to tighten all procurement operations, resulting in recentralization and greater top-down control permeating the federal government's activities. Some might call part of this a mindless overreaction, driven by the fear of being blamed—a pervasive if unintended negative side effect—but in any case one can argue that things managerial were not necessarily largely resolved or as in hand as one might like.

SPECIAL CIRCUMSTANCES?

It has been argued that the exposition of this fiasco does not require fundamental structural adjustment of Canadian governance because such abnormal times are unlikely to recur and because the normal processes, in this case, were unduly and uncharacteristically strained. The close result of the 1995 referendum meant that the federal government of the day set about trying to convince Canadians (especially Quebeckers) of the benefits of maintaining a united Canada.

The prime minister at the time took a personal interest, and the overall strategy that was designed and implemented

worked on a need-to-know basis. This strategy weakened
the process of due diligence. Senior public servants who
were not directly involved avoided commenting on or even
finding out what was going on. In other words, the customary
camaraderie among deputy ministers that extends to informal
backstopping for each other may not have been in play to the
same extent as usual.

Unfortunately, at the same time, there was evidence of poor
management and inconsistent oversight (Gomery 2004). In
particular, the management of sponsorship initiatives, and
of the subsequent Sponsorship Program (in existence from
November 1997 to August 31, 2001), was poorly designed
and executed during the critical period following the
referendum. This is especially true given the (legitimate)
political involvement in event selection and the consequential
increased perceptions of risk to management safeguards.

Notwithstanding any special circumstances, it is a deputy
minister's duty to be informed about administration and
management within his department, especially in these
complex and fluid circumstances, given the expenditures
involved ($130 million from November 1997 to September
2001 for the Sponsorship Program), although any judgment
of the deputy minister's actions must be tempered by the fact
that he had other responsibilities (e.g., other procurements,
real estate, downsizing, etc.). PWGSC spends $10 billion in
procurement in a typical year, and the deputy minister had
20,000 employees in the period before 1995. Deputy ministers'
responsibilities have recently been described as comprising
"sound public service advice on policy development and
implementation ... ; effective departmental management;
and as well as advice on management of the Minister's entire
portfolio, fulfillment of authorities ... assigned to the DM or
other department officials ... " (GOC 2003a).

So it seems to be reasonable to expect that it is the duty
of the deputy minister to inform the Privy Council Office
(including the clerk, as required) of any concerns (e.g., any

malaise that Quail may have felt about the de facto reporting relationships involving one of his employees). Indeed, the recently released Guidance to Deputy Ministers explains that when a deputy minister is not able to achieve the required balance in accountabilities or encounters matters that "the Deputy Minister considers significant enough to affect their accountabilities, those of their Minister, or the agenda and direction of government ... ," she is expected to consult the clerk of the Privy Council (GOC 2003a).

But these obligations remain couched in such general terms and have little bite. Ran Quail, a respected, experienced, and able deputy minister, appears not to have met these obligations. One is entitled to ask why. Indeed, one may legitimately ask, how could this have been? From a public management point of view, the failure to be as fully informed as a deputy minister should, together with the failure to communicate with the clerk on a matter of such sensitivity, reveals breaks in communication within the higher levels of the public service that might be regarded as astonishing.

GOOD MANAGEMENT AND INTELLIGENT ACCOUNTABILITY

This case highlights the requirement both for good management and for intelligent accountability. The first requirement—the duty to be informed—pertains to the sort of routine safeguards required within the bureaucracy to prevent anyone from taking inappropriate advantage of government contracting and administrative procedures. The second requirement—the duty to inform—deals with accountability for wrongdoing in our parliamentary system of governance and takes into account the important boundary between the bureaucracy and politicians (the executive and Parliament).

There is obviously a need to improve administrative procedures to strengthen safeguards against inappropriate advantage being taken of government contracting. These are matters of routine management. But they raise serious questions about the extent to which a deputy minister should be responsible for ensuring that he is fully informed even about such routine procedures. Over the years, the minister has been held less and less responsible for such monitoring. While he has been held accountable by Parliament, he has not been asked to accept culpability for the deeds of employees who work there, nor has he been required to be fully informed of how these employees dispatch their work.

It is much less clear that the deputy minister can be absolved of the responsibility for work being done as it should be. Indeed, if the deputy minister's duty is not to be informed of the minutiae of the work of his department, and for the design and maintenance of an information system that will ensure that he is fully informed, the whole process of administration is in question.

More important, though, are the deputy minister's accountability mechanisms in our parliamentary system of governance. The deputy minister is primarily accountable not only to his minister, to the Treasury Board, and to the prime minister, and through them to cabinet and Parliament, but also for public governance as embodied in the public service system and as a result, through the clerk of the Privy Council (as head of the public service), to Canadian citizens and the Parliament that represents them. In other words, the deputy minister has a duty to inform that is as important as his responsibility to be informed.

While speaking truth to power is usually interpreted in a narrow way as a duty to inform and advise the minister fairly and fully, it should be clear that this is too narrow a view. The clerk of the Privy Council, as both head of the public service and the bureaucratic conduit to the prime minister of the day, is also entitled to be fully and fairly informed. Failing to do so can only be interpreted as a dereliction of duty by the deputy minister.

On both fronts, the real accountability of deputy ministers seems to be fading away too. In fact, this erosion may have been fostered by the adversarialism of the formal Canadian system of governance. But whatever the reason, there appears to be a growing general failure to accept responsibility and a refusal to accept culpability and liability.

And it is something that appears to be seeping into official thinking. As expert witness C. E. S. Franks put it, in testifying to the Public Accounts Committee about the sponsorship affair, "Not one of the many witnesses who came before the committee, neither ex-ministers nor public servants, ever stated: 'yes, managing this program was my responsibility, and I am responsible and accountable for whatever went wrong with it'" (2004, 64).

EVASIVE THINKING ABOUT REPAIRS

When faced with crises, there is a natural propensity to escape through "evasive thinking," as Vaclav Havel would call it. This is a propensity to bring the issue to a higher level of abstraction as a way to theorize and pontificate about process without paying much attention to practical issues. Such disquisitions, like sixteenth-century maps, are elegant but not very helpful to navigation. Havel (1991, 10–24) illustrates this propensity to indulge in evasive thinking by the way in which the communist press in Eastern Europe was prone to deal with the practical problem of window ledges falling from buildings in Prague and killing or wounding pedestrians. The press did not call for repairs but was quite pleased to celebrate the extraordinary freedom of the press in Prague, where newspapers were allowed to talk about falling window ledges.

On the operational front, there is nothing wrong with setting out what is expected (e.g., the government's Guidance for Deputy Ministers and Values and Ethics Code) and devising rational frameworks for managing, like the Treasury Board's

2003 Management Accountability Framework. And there is no doubt that the intent of these frameworks is to guide *what should be done*. But it is important to reflect on whether asserting that they are in place is actually going to translate into the right kind of difference being made to daily actions and behaviour.

The government's response (as set out in GOC 2005) to Parliament's Public Accounts Committee (PAC) looks at the sponsorship affair in this light. The committee made four recommendations that centred on the adoption of the accounting officer idea as a way of strengthening accountability to Parliament. The government's approach was, understandably, very general to avoid dealing with the specific recommendations. It simply denied that ambiguity exists in the current system with respect to the assignment of accountability either generally or to the deputy minister (neatly sidestepping the issue of Franks' observations that the way things are currently viewed officially means that no one seems to hold accountability for what happened). And the government opposed any strengthening of the link between deputies and Parliament beyond what exists today as inappropriate, unnecessary, or unworkable because of strong negative consequences. The government then proceeded to lecture the committee on what has been or is being put in place (e.g., the MAF) to clarify expectations, assess performance, and mete out sanctions and to describe how these initiatives will be used.

The desire to fend off public blame and to keep harsh critics at bay appears to be overcoming any need to find creative paths to improvement. In fact, the term "plausible deniability" comes to mind as the main driver of actions and behaviour throughout the review of this debacle.

In that sense, the comments of John Williams, chair of the PAC (*Ottawa Citizen*, August 24, 2005) hit the nail on the head: what is so wrong about requiring "a deputy minister to advise the Clerk of Privy Council and the auditor general when asked by his minister to do anything unethical or inappropriate? If one were to make the deputy minister an accounting officer to Parliament, the excuse 'the deputy minister was not in the loop' would never again be acceptable."

On the theoretical front, evasive thinking and a certain taste for metaphysics are also making headway. Scholars such as Aucoin and Jarvis (2005) and others tackling the issue of accountability insist on the need to modernize it by addressing its broad, diffuse, and intractable aspects. Aucoin and Jarvis recommend giving higher importance to the parliamentary scrutiny of ministers and officials, improving a deputy minister's accountability to Parliament, strengthening public service independence by altering the regime for selecting deputy ministers, enhancing parliamentary scrutiny through independent performance reviews carried out by a new agency, and extending the accountability regime further for crown corporations. The addition of deputy ministers' direct accountability to Parliament for areas for which they are explicitly responsible (as Aucoin and Jarvis suggest) may be helpful in a general way, but it is unlikely to help avoid a recurrence of the mishaps experienced in cases such as the sponsorship affair.

The logic of both the operational and the theoretical arguments leads to the multiplication of control mechanisms, some of which are likely to be not only onerous administratively but also insufficient if not entirely futile when it comes to providing effective accountability. They all constitute attempts either to use system-wide control or to salvage a pure Westminster model that no longer fits reality by propping it up in a manner likely to be as effective as dressing the man next door in a pilot's uniform and pretending that he can fly a CF-18.

A MATTER OF INCENTIVES

While one may applaud the new timid and general "guide-lines," they are unlikely to prevent the reoccurrence of this sorry mess. A better fail-safe solution must be found. Good behaviour cannot be legislated.

In the complex, fluid, fast-moving fish bowl environment in which deputy ministers function, it is incentives that matter and influence judgment and action. Given the blurring of the administrative/political boundary that can only be exacerbated in some cases, as in crises that push the political/administrative system into improvisation territory, we believe that useful improvements can be made by focusing on the link between the deputy minister and the executive and reinforcing her duties to be informed and to inform. These duties are implicit in the new accountability regime, recently introduced in the public service. For us, however, that duty has to be translated into a simple mechanism that provides the right incentives and has some bite.

Our suggestion is simple: make use of the letters that deputy ministers usually receive from the clerk of the Privy Council when they are appointed to a new set of responsibilities. This document generally includes in broad terms the highlighting of areas of particular emphasis for the forthcoming period, including policy and/or management-administration. The clerk can additionally set out in every such letter the duties of the deputy ministers (1) to be informed (about the management and administration within their departments) and (2) to inform both the clerk and the minister (about difficulties in management and administration within their departments), as they deem appropriate. This approach would strengthen the incentive to err on the side of making sure. As well, the letter should set out stiff sanctions for failure to comply with these informational requirements. Deputy ministers generally serve "at pleasure," so failure to perform one or both of these fundamental duties could entail immediate dismissal from the ranks of deputy ministers and therefore from the ranks of the public service.

This is not unlike suggestions that have been made about changes in company law to ensure that those concerned are reminded that they are granted the privilege of operating an incorporated limited liability company by the state, that it is a privilege granted by the state under certain conditions, and that, if these conditions are not met, the state can withdraw these privileges (Paquet 2005c, Chapter 11).

CONCLUSION

We do not intend in this chapter to give a definitive solution to the thorny problem of senior public servants' accountability. We simply suggest that a tiny bit of organizational *bricolage* might do a lot of good. We have used insights gleaned from reflecting on the sponsorship scandal to devise practical solutions aimed at bringing about real change in a dynamic, complex, and adaptive system.

Some consider that the problem of deputy ministers' accountability has already been resolved. Others have proposed a massive overhaul of the command-and-control role of Parliament. Both views take refuge in system-wide, top-down initiatives and/or idealistic generalities that are unlikely to be very helpful in the here and now.

Deputy ministers are neither pure, selfless knights nor entirely self-interested knaves (Le Grand 2003): they are rational human beings who are probably more reasonable and honest than the average citizen (given the screening that they go through), and they are influenced in their decision making and behaviour by incentives. Ignoring these incentives, not recognizing that making plausible deniability easier may hinder robust action on certain fronts, and not using the full panoply of incentive reward systems (with all their subtlety) in defining deputy ministers' mandate may be nothing less than criminal negligence.

Whether a significant change in the letter of guidance to deputy ministers might have prevented the worst excesses of the sponsorship affair is difficult to demonstrate. Our sense,

however, is that it would have. This will remain what Jacques
Lesourne calls one of "ces avenirs qui n'ont pas eu lieu"
(2003).

GOMERY I:

FLAWED FROM THE BEGINNING

> Ses plus grandes œuvres sont des cauchemars de scrupuleux rédigés par un ironiste et par un roi de la parabole sur un ton de procès-verbal.
> —Alexandre Vialatte (1998), à propos de Kafka

INTRODUCTION

It may seem a little incongruous to refer to Kafka when analyzing the first report of Justice John Gomery on the sponsorship affair. Yet this report has a Kafkaesque flavour. As his journal attests, Kafka was often distraught and even led, on one occasion, to divide a sheet of paper into two columns to try to decide whether or not to marry—the reasons for doing so in one column and those for not doing so in the other. This exercise had nothing to do with the joy or the grief brought by marriage; it had to do with Kafka's anguish and self-blame over his inability to love. All of Kafka's work springs from this guilt. In the same way, Gomery's work is bound to echo his circumstances. Gomery brought some baggage to the task along with a certain mindset. Reports of commissions of inquiry never spring to life fully formed.

First, Gomery is a judge. He has been trained to adjudicate and to find guilt or innocence, and he can no more escape from this reality than a turtle can leave its shell. He is neither an organizational design specialist nor an expert in political philosophy or public administration. As a result, he appears to have been ill prepared to untangle the underlying strands of the sponsorship affair.

Second, Gomery is an Anglo-Quebecker who, as Douglas Fisher has suggested (2005), is permeated by the mindset of his fellow Anglo-Quebeckers. Since the 1970s, they have remained obsessed with the view in good currency in Westmount at the time that, faced with the threat of the Quebec sovereignty movement, the best remedy — perhaps the only remedy — was and remains the Trudeau-like, intransigent, federal Liberal Party's imposing its own rule top down.

Gomery embodied these two handicaps in a particularly toxic way. He was given a job that seemed to be relatively simple: to establish the facts. But doing that well would have required a reasonable grasp of the context from which these facts emerged. However, in defining the context, Gomery made some basic choices that sent his report in directions that cannot necessarily be defended and seem a little Kafkaesque. Indeed, for Gomery, the sponsorship affair was a sort of Rorschach test. His report was therefore bound to echo his own assumptions as much as an objective picture of external reality.

First, Gomery chose to define his mandate in political terms — recently declaring that he had chosen Bernard Roy (a former political lieutenant of Brian Mulroney) as principal prosecutor because he wanted to avoid being labelled as an acolyte of the federal Liberals.

Second, he chose to surround himself with advisers who had a particularly strong centralist view of the Canadian political system and who, as a result, helped to reinforce his view of things. Understandably, he was then led to build his report on a number of presumptions, such as the continued relevance of a pure Westminster-type responsible government regime in Canada.

And third, Gomery chose both to apportion blame and to bestow exoneration on specific people, which he did not have to do. To do this, he had to make further assumptions: about the nature of the workings of the governmental apparatus, about the nature of accountability, and about the nature of the elements that could form the basis of determining blame and innocence.

On all of these fronts, the choices that he made were questionable, and as a result his conclusions need to be taken with a grain of salt. Even more serious is that, having made these choices, he did not stick to them consistently. He abandoned his presumptions and assumptions when it suited him. He would like to be able to say, like the judge-penitent of Albert Camus, "Chez moi, on ne bénit pas, on ne distribue pas d'absolution. On fait l'addition, simplement ... ," but he proved himself incapable of doing this (Camus 1956).

GOMERY AND WESTMINSTER

There is no consensus on the continued reality of a pure Westminster model in Canada. Some believe that it still exists, while others see it as a ghost of the past, as something that continues to survive only in the fantasy world of theorists. Close advisers persuaded Gomery to defend the dominium of Westminster. As a result, he affirmed that the minister is accountable before Parliament for the actions of her subordinates, even when their actions flow from responsibilities delegated to them by the Treasury Board or the Public Service Commission. Consequently, he refused to accept a separation between what is political and what is administrative, and he exonerated most senior officials save in a few particular cases (e.g., Guité seriously and Quail tokenly).

As a result, Gomery, even though he wanted to focus on "political accountability" when determining who should be held accountable for the sponsorship initiative's blunders, could not hold to the presumption of a fundamentally pure Westminster regime in existence—because the testimonies that he heard show that it does not correspond to the Canadian reality.

Over the years, as the complexity and size of the state have grown, ministerial responsibility has been attenuated. Reg Alcock, the former president of the Treasury Board, observed when he tabled his new policy on management control in October 2005 that ministerial responsibility "does not mean that the minister must accept blame whenever something goes wrong in his or her department. Accountability and blame are different: blame applies only if problems are attributable to the inappropriate action or inaction of the minister" (cited in Clark 2005). Alcock was just saying out loud what all the serious government watchers have known for a long time. It is unrealistic to believe that a minister can monitor all activities in departments that employ many thousands of bureaucrats, where technical details abound, and where different rules are needed in different circumstances. Nor is it reasonable to hold her responsible for all the things that go wrong. She must explain them in the House of Commons but cannot really be held responsible for them.

Consequently, Gomery could not blame only ministers. He was reduced to casting blame on a whole range of people — ministers and bureaucrats. But since the inquiry that he led did not in most cases shed light on individual responsibility cleanly and clearly, and since he was frequently unable to shine a light clearly on who was responsible for the blunders ("nothing is proven" is an expression that crops up often in the text but does not seem to halt his urgent need to draw conclusions), he often had to decide about allocating responsibility and blameworthiness without much on which to make such a judgment.

For example, Gomery had to determine how much blame should fall on the shoulders of Minister Gagliano and how much on those of Ran Quail, his deputy minister, for what seems to have been significant negligence in the oversight of the Sponsorship Program. On what basis, furthermore, could

Gomery decide who, among the people working for the prime minister (Gagliano's boss) or the clerk of the Privy Council (Quail's boss), should accept blame for not knowing what was going on? Gomery seldom had direct evidence: he had only contradictory versions of the facts, and presumptions about the weighting of such evidence, to help him parse the portions of "truth" out of the fragments that were available.

As a result, there had to be a certain degree of improvisation and caprice when Gomery chose to blame some people and to exonerate others, all the while holding to the fundamentally pure version of Westminster, but not really able to hold to it, because he was not ready to cling to it in what appeared to be a sensible and constant way. Gomery, in front of his piece of paper, agonized about whether he should marry or not!

GOMERY AND THE
PALIMPSEST OF ACCOUNTABILITY

Just as Gomery had a very hazy idea of government apparatus, so too his grasp of accountability was somewhat shaky. Because everyone seems to be partly responsible up to a certain point, the result is a grey zone. It is in circumstances like these that the loose rules of a public inquiry carry so much weight.

Instead of conducting his inquiry so as to understand the working of an organization that has become derailed, to take the cogs of the system to pieces, and to define the logic that brought about the skidding off the rails, Gomery mainly sought incriminating statements in the public hearings. In this great expedition, proof was poorly defined, and interrogation was more or less conclusive, depending on the degree to which the witnesses were pressed. Some questioning turned out to be a flagrant indulgence of witnesses; in other cases, it was very pointed.

Some actions may have been wrong according to the usual contracting procedures, and some practices (e.g., overcharging, charging for non-existent work, or commissions paid to the Liberal Party by contractors) seem to have been frankly dishonest. Nevertheless, it is difficult to dissect the decision-making processes into tiny slices, hoping to decide as a result which was the key to the whole thing going pear shaped, or to say to what extent these various decision-making steps were deliberate defrauding of the government rather than simply the result of a poor fit of the usual rules (i.e., being overly restrictive) or simply their being unworkable, as Guité said.

In a time of presumed crisis, showing that public servants tried to take shortcuts and allowed their bad habits to bloom does not show that there was an explicit conspiracy. The result was certainly that a decision-making process that tried to cut corners, together with dishonest actions, produced results that were much more serious than anyone had anticipated. But which blunder in which part of the decision-making process lies at the heart of the disaster?

In his book *The Logic of Failure,* Dietrich Dörner (1997) shows that in the Chernobyl case, it was impossible to point the finger at any one person for the disaster: a collection of people indulged in bad practices or exercised poor judgment, but none of them could be identified as the single determining factor. Nevertheless, the sum total led to the central nuclear station's meltdown.

The responsibility is even harder to identify when one deals not only with sins of commission (i.e., the blunders that resulted from the deliberate actions of specific people) but also with sins of omission (*une insouciance déréglée ou téméraire,* an "unsettling or rash lack of concern," to use the characterization of the Criminal Code in describing negligent behaviour, a pattern of inaction that is not up to the expected standard of a professional). For sins of commission (fraud, fake bills, illegal commissions, etc.), it is usually easy to pinpoint the blame. A visible act was committed, so it is possible to say that so and so was the source of the problem. For sins of omission, on the other hand, things are more complicated.

Who should have known what would probably be a mistake? Under which conditions can one speak of "unsettling or rash lack of concern"? In the case of a decision-making process that is cloaked in shadows, on what basis can one determine who "ought to have known" and "ought to have acted"? An organizational design specialist, like a plumber, must start with the evidence of failure and work his way back up to the source of the problem.

Gomery blamed some and exonerated others often on the basis of shaky proofs—*evidence lite,* to quote an often-used term. It is important to remember that the idea of proof, what is called evidence, is much less rigorous in the world of judicial inquiries than in the corridors of formal justice. One of these "inquiries" a couple of decades ago blamed Minister Sinclair Stevens for misbehaviour only to have a real court of law, using *"real proof,"* exonerate him years later (unfortunately when the damage had already been done).

In the name of prudence, it might be wiser in many cases when there is a lack of proof to attribute blame to a system rather than to individuals, but in this case that did not happen. In his determination to allocate blame more precisely, Gomery chose to anthropomorphize the process by creating good and bad people. It was only in his second report (Gomery II) that he was supposed to identify bad habits and routines and propose ways of correcting them. In the meantime, Gomery I identified those whom he thought were worthy of blame and gave benedictions and absolutions to others.

GOMERY AND BLAME-ABILITY

It is one of the professional burdens of judges to decide who is guilty and who is innocent. But in the courts of justice, the rules are clear. Everyone is presumed innocent until proven guilty, and proof must be established beyond a reasonable doubt. It must be clear that the actions of the accused were the cause of the harm. The head of an inquiry might be a judge, but he does not work under these constraints. As a result, Justice Gomery was free to do much damage. He allocated blame and exoneration in a way that is hard to understand. In certain cases, he identified sins of commission, and justice followed its logical path. In other cases, he chose to identify sins of omission supposedly committed by "unsettling or rash lack of concern" when other similar sins were not condemned.

In the case of an organization accused of negligence, legal theory says that the identification of blame depends on the spirit of the organization at the moment that the act was committed. One examines the guiding principles of the organization and compares them to those of a reasonable organization placed in the same circumstances. This is where Gomery's margin of manoeuvrability came into play.

It is difficult to assume that Paul Martin had no information that was pertinent to the sponsorship file, bearing in mind the testimony of Allan Cutler, who tabled a document (dated January 26, 1996) with the Gomery Commission in which he claimed to have brought to the attention of his superiors and raised questions about an amendment of $909,000 to a contract with Groupe Everest for work done for the Department of Finance (when Martin was minister of finance). The questions raised by Cutler had to do with the fact that this amendment was a retroactive one in which Groupe Everest would likely receive a commission for the subcontract without necessarily having done any work. In the same way, it is difficult to assume that the clerk of the Privy Council was entirely in the dark about what was going on when it is known from the testimonies at the Gomery inquiry that the associate secretary to cabinet (and principal associate to the clerk), Ron Bilodeau, had telephoned Ran Quail (the deputy minister of Public Works and Government Services) at the end of 1996 or the beginning of 1997 to tell him that one of his assistant deputy ministers (Jim Stobbe) was asking too many questions of Chuck Guité on the subject of the activities of the Sponsorship Program and to let him know that this questioning was not welcome. As well, it is difficult to understand how and why, in the face of contradictory testimony, Gomery chose to believe Guité (the civil servant) rather than Jean Pelletier (the secretary to the prime minister).

Of course, Justice Gomery had the right to choose whom he believed, and whom he did not, and to condemn and absolve whom he wished, but these were the opinions of one person, his determinations were founded on certain presumptions, and his decisions cannot be explained in a way that seems to be reasonable and credible to third parties (as they should).

In making such choices in important matters, one can use three different standards: "nothing but the truth," "the whole truth," and "a certain plausibility." Using the first standard, one would use as the basis of judgment only those facts that have been definitely confirmed and proven beyond reasonable doubt, and one would exclude anything that was in the least uncertain. The second standard goes further and draws a larger circle that includes a good number of uncertainties and conjectures that have not been "proven beyond all doubt." The third goes further still, permitting a greater degree of speculation and leaving more room for imagination.

As Steve Fuller (2005) suggests in his book *The Intellectual,* judicial power commonly uses the first standard. Legislatures, on the other hand, often allow themselves to search for the "whole truth"—that is, going beyond the small circle of what is proven beyond all doubt. As a result, legislatures use standards that are more lax and more inclusive than "nothing but the truth" when they define what they call "facts." In the case of Gomery, it is clear that he went even further still, allowing himself to base his decisions on a certain degree of "plausibility."

The consequence is that Gomery I may be said to suffer from dangerous laxity at the exact moment of determining who should have known and who did not speak up loudly enough.

CONCLUSION

One should not conclude from this analysis that everything in the first Gomery report is unacceptable. The commission established many facts beyond doubt. And one has since seen fraud charges in a number of cases.

One can also assume that the analyses of Gomery I led Gomery II to propose a certain number of reforms in the decision-making processes of the state. But these recommendations, made as they were in the faint glow of collective and localized blunders, may simply stultify the system and add unreasonably to the controls without engendering an intelligent, strengthened accountability. So we do not have reason to be very optimistic (Hubbard and Paquet 2005; Paquet 2004a, 2004b, 2005b).

Notwithstanding some potential positive features, however, one can already conclude that Gomery I was a failure at two levels. First, it was built on a great number of questionable presumptions in his inquiry, so there was a certain degree of capriciousness in what should have been a document that stuck scrupulously to "nothing but the truth." Second, Gomery's perspective remained quite reductive throughout the inquiry. Gomery adamantly refused to comment on the underlying source of the affair, one that goes to the heart of Canadian federalism: up to what point is it legitimate in a democracy for a party in power, one that is supposed to govern in the name of the entire population (of a province or a country), to use public funds for marketing activities aimed at convincing people that one particular voting option or cause is the best?

In the first case, Gomery seems to have botched up his work. It is by no means certain that the report's credibility escaped damage as a result of the paradoxical combination of boldness and timidity that Justice Gomery chose to display *selon les circonstances*. He chose to accuse some players without proof but to appeal, in some inexplicable way, to a *devoir de réserve* in order to absolve some players over and over—people whom it is difficult to believe were not "in the know."

In the second case, the problem remains unnoticed and thus unaddressed. The Liberal Party of Canada (LPC) continued to market its point of view (the unity of Canada at any price, like it or not) with the support of public money from the taxes of many people who do not share this view. The Parti Québécois did the same thing when it was in power in Quebec. In either case, it doesn't seem to matter that an important part of the electorate (for good reason or not) does not support the point of view being marketed.

It was not sufficient for Justice Gomery to establish whether the sponsorship funds were spent in an administratively inappropriate way; he was also required to decide whether they were spent legally (according to the law) and legitimately (in a democracy like ours). It is not unreasonable to say that the Liberal Party of Canada not only affirmed its intent to impose national unity but also wanted to impose it under conditions that it asserts are desirable (i.e., a strongly centralized regime). From this, it seems to follow for the LPC that every method of persuasion seemed to be legal and legitimate for defending this cause, even to the point of justifying distortions of the law or making use of disinformation, untruths, intimidation, or deception.

The same logic ought to apply as the one that controls electoral spending by the party in power (federal or provincial): the one that forbids that party to use public money—money that was given to the state by citizens who do not necessarily share the view of that party and that was given exclusively for other uses (e.g., the provision of goods and services in the public good)—to promote its own electoral interests. These rules exist to prevent abuse analogous to that investigated by the Gomery inquiry. However, this is a minefield into which Justice Gomery—for obscure reasons that may have to do with the baggage that he brought with him—did not have the courage to venture.

GOMERY II:

FEAR OF BLURRING AND LACK OF

TEMPERANTIA

Je comptais sur ses doigts et je me suis trompé.
—Jim Corcoran (2005)

INTRODUCTION

Justice John Gomery's phase one report, *Who Is Responsible?* (Gomery I), filed in November 2005, landed like a grenade. His phase two report, *Restoring Accountability: Recommendations* (Gomery II), filed in February 2006, generated more of a whimper than a bang. Reforming is not as entertaining as publicly blaming. Yet the repercussions of the ideas put forward in Gomery II on the mode of governing in Canada may well be significant, so they deserve some critical attention.

Pessimists anticipated that Gomery II would be limited to suggesting some adjustments to the machinery of government in order to improve it marginally; optimists saw the Gomery inquiry as a potential *glasnost* that would throw some light on poor governance processes and prepare a wished-for *perestroika* of Canadian federalism (Paquet 2005a). At the end of the day, the recommendations of Gomery II are neither as trivial as feared nor as inspiring as hoped for.

A great weakness of the report is its failure to factor in the challenges of governance in a world in which power, resources, and information are now widely distributed. While this new reality has been recognized in some of the background research studies of the commission of inquiry (Roberts 2006), it is not a feature of the Gomery II report itself.

In this kind of world, coordination and collaboration are crucial requirements, both at the political-administrative interface and horizontally among the different players. This occlusion has allowed a romanticized view of the public administration system to prevail. A mindset has taken hold in the report that has determined that firewalls have to be built everywhere, despite the existence of a world of governance that calls for continuous collaboration, social learning, and much blurring of roles (Thacher and Rein 2004). As a result, Gomery II is an amalgam of useful if general and banal recommendations, along with others that are seriously wrong-headed.

This emerging world of collaboration must also be able to count on fail-safe mechanisms and crucial mavens who accumulate information and knowledge about many dimensions of the governing process. Such features are essential to ensure that the system does not fall prey to saboteurs and will be able, when needed, to generate innovative, reasonable, and negotiated arrangements that are likely to receive general support. As a result, it is crucial to maintain the conditions necessary for the government of the day to govern effectively and creatively. Gomery, in his second report, does not appear to have understood this point.

A FOCUS ON BLAME

Gomery I's diagnosis is built on the judge's personal choices about which evidence to accept and on his judgments about culpability (Gomery 2005, 3). Gomery II also focuses "on the need to pinpoint who is responsible when things go wrong, and who is to blame" (Gomery 2006, 9). To do so, Gomery II becomes obsessively preoccupied with defining the roles and responsibilities of the different political officials and senior public servants (especially deputy ministers) precisely so that it is clear where the finger should be pointed when things go wrong.

Gomery I is contentious because it appears not to provide a sufficiently rich and substantive base of evidence to persuasively support many of its conclusions, especially with respect to assigning blame and exoneration (Paquet 2006a). Gomery II is proving to be equally contentious because, in the context of complex and ever-changing social systems such as Canadian governance, interconnectedness and interactions are always present, and pinpointing responsibility may be not only difficult but also outright misguided. Things may have gone wrong not as a result of any one person's deeds or misdeeds but as the result of a constellation of innocuous elements or bad habits that have developed over time in a system (Dorner 1997). Indeed, Gomery's obsession with pinpointing blame and apportioning punishment (or enabling its apportionment) generated significant flaws in both reports.

Gomery was additionally hampered in preparing his second report (as he himself admits) by his lack of knowledge and experience in public administration. As a result, he decided to put in place a research program as well as a broad consultation initiative guided by an advisory committee and to lean heavily on a special adviser, Donald Savoie, a public administration expert. The majority of the research team, and certainly the special adviser himself, are on the record as strong believers in the existing parliamentary system: they have bemoaned the overcentralization of power at the executive level, and around the office of the prime minister of the day (which has weakened Parliament's role), and the disappearance of a neat compartmentalization of politics and administration.

The literature on public administration is in general less fundamentalist and much more nuanced on many of these issues than the Savoie team. Even Savoie himself noted a few years ago that "we may well have reached the point where accountability—in the sense of retrospectively blaming individuals or even departments for problems—is no longer possible or fair" and that we may no longer be in a world where "the line of command is the same as the line of responsibility" (2003, 268, 269).

Yet these nuances are all absent in Gomery II. They remain in somewhat subdued form in some of the research studies but have vanished completely from the official report. Interestingly, Sharon Sutherland, one of the researchers, has called the report "foolish" and taken particular issue with "changing the rules to handicap the institutions that do work" (May 2006a). The urge in Gomery II to pinpoint blame seems to trump both reality and clear thinking.

A TASTE FOR BLACK-AND-WHITE DEMARCATIONS AND FORMALISM

Gomery II's recommendations fall into four main categories: defining the roles and responsibilities of key players as clearly as possible; arming "Parliament and its agents" with stronger levers and additional resources to make them a more effective counterforce to government (i.e., the executive); constraining the power of the prime minister; and giving public servants more protection to withstand inappropriate pressure from the government of the day. As well, Gomery II suggests changing the current definition of "government advertising" to conform to advertising industry standards. The report also requests that the government report to Parliament within twenty-four months on how it has dealt with these recommendations.

Some recommendations (i.e., the idea that ministers not be called to the Public Accounts Committee [PAC] as a rule) are puzzling. As some experienced former deputy ministers such as Arthur Kroeger (2006) have pointed out, ministers rarely attend PAC meetings anyway. Providing more resources to parliamentary committees, especially the PAC, and reducing turnover in their membership are simply good management, but to the extent that a new culture of accountability of deputy ministers (rather than simple answerability) is developed it can drive a sharp wedge between ministers and deputy ministers. So some recommendations seem to be somewhat banal but could turn out to be disruptive.

An example of a recommendation that might not be helpful in practice because it goes too far is one that echoes the view that *maxima are optima*: if some transparency is good, then more must be better. Gomery II recommends that public servants be obliged to keep a paper trail of all their decisions and recommendations. Since a great deal of paperwork must already be kept, adding to it may be excessive.

Other recommendations (individually or taken together) are not simply unworkable but in fact destructive. For example, dismembering the current role of the clerk would entail a major weakening of the government of the day, since the clerk is called upon to ensure that the Public Service Commission, the Prime Minister's Office, and cabinet are working in concert. Dismantling this institution would turn the clock back almost to the 1930s, when the clerk was little more than a registrar (Hubbard and Paquet 2006a). Indeed, given the centrality of this coordinating function, it is difficult to understand why Gomery II suggests such a thing and why it chooses to say so little about the consequences of such dismantling or about the disconcertation likely to ensue.

In the matter of strengthening the link between deputy ministers and Parliament, Gomery II is careful to argue (like the PAC and the 1979 Lambert Commission report before it) that there is no intent to have the PAC mete out punishment or give instructions to the deputy ministers and senior officials who would appear before it in their own right. Nevertheless, it is hard to imagine that Canada's PAC would be able to resist the temptation to play partisan politics and to press for public punishment when mistakes are uncovered.

Even more strangely, having made the point about the importance of maintaining deputy ministers' accountability to the government, Gomery's fourth recommendation can be argued to be suggesting precisely the opposite by stating that the government should explicitly "acknowledge and declare that Deputy Ministers and senior public servants who have statutory responsibility are accountable in their own right for statutory and delegated responsibilities before the Public Accounts Committee" (Gomery 2006, 100). In fact, this is the interpretation made in an open letter to Prime Minister Harper, signed by a large number of luminaries from the private, public, and not-for-profit sectors, that was prepared in late February 2006 and sent in early March (May 2006b).

Thus, while some of Gomery II's recommendations may do some good, the sum total would amount to reducing the capacity of the government of the day to govern; increasing the power of the parliamentary committees; increasing the power and independence of the bureaucracy; and freezing the processes of administration and stultifying the process of social learning that is rooted in continuous interaction between the bureaucracy and the government of the day.

One point is clear. The rebalancing of power that would ensue from full implementation of Gomery II's recommendations would undoubtedly increase the power of Parliament somewhat but would increase the power of the unelected bureaucracy even further, to the detriment of the government of the day. Indeed, one might boldly compare the impact of Gomery II's being fully implemented to a hijacking of the administrative process by the bureaucracy—not dissimilar to the way that the Charter of Rights and Freedoms handed more power to the judiciary. Full implementation of the recommendations of Gomery II would entail a drift toward what Arthur Kroeger calls "government by the unelected" (May 2006b).

Such a shift of power toward the bureaucracy flows from a determination to avoid any blurring of roles and responsibilities: firewalls and formal rules are inflicted on the public administration system, without much concern for the elected officials' core governing responsibilities, which need to be carried out in concert with bureaucratic officials. The excessive sanitization of the processes proposed by Gomery II would entail an attenuation of the role of elected officials in the governance of the country and the creation of an administrative state that might tend to neutralize the work of the government while pretending to provide Parliament with greater real powers.

BETWEEN GOVERNMENT-OF-THE-DAY PHOBIA AND THE WESTMINSTER DOCTRINE

The analysis of the Gomery Commission focused almost exclusively on the misdeeds of a few bureaucrats and a few private sector firms that seized the occasion of a national crisis to exploit weaknesses of the administrative processes. The likelihood of such a configuration of circumstances occurring again is so low, as Gomery himself has stated, that one can legitimately ask why it would be useful to modify the whole process of public administration just to deal explicitly with such an unlikely event. One would have expected from Gomery II a less simplistic analysis and a more reflective inquiry into why the system failed and suggestions of what should be done to make it work better. Two sets of forces prevented the Gomery Commission from providing that kind of reframing and from drawing from it some inspiration for a better design.

First, an excessively narrow focus on what could have prevented the particular misdeeds rather than on the overall malfunctioning of the system that generated them had an impact on the contents of Gomery I. Having indicted two key players of the government of the day in Gomery I (Jean Chrétien and Jean Pelletier), the inquiry was led in Gomery II to focus on clipping the government's wings. This mission led to a flurry of proposals to contain the government of the day by strengthening Parliament and the bureaucracy, thereby potentially crippling the capacity of the party in power to govern.

Second, one should not underestimate the power of ideas. It is the strong view in some quarters of academe that Parliament should rule and that the administrative bureaucracy (the public service, including deputy ministers) should carry out the orders.

The Gomery II research team provided some artillery to rationalize this stylization of an ideal Manichean world. Using the language of Le Grand (2003), the implicit assumption behind that stylization is that all politicians *who are not part* of the government of the day, and all public servants, are *knights* (i.e., people who act out of the interests of others even to the detriment of their own interests), while all politicians *who are part* of the government (and their acolytes) are *knaves* (i.e., not bad people but people who act out of their own best interests).

Both these forces derailed the inquiry. The urge to neuter the government of the day, and the view that politics/policy and administration can no more mix than water and oil, led Gomery II to suggest firewalls where coordination is required.

The criticisms should not be construed as denying that there may be problems in these areas in the federal public household: the federal Liberal government has obviously overcentralized power in the hands of the executive; at times, there have been some undue small-p political interventions in the administrative processes; and the clerk has not always exercised his key gubernatorial functions well and wisely, in a maven-like way.

The federal Liberal government has been in denial vis-à-vis the transformation of governance that has seen power effectively leaking upward, downward, and sideways from central governments. So its knee-jerk reaction has been a strategy of additional centralization at all costs, producing not only ineffective governance and poor productivity but also legitimate resentment and sovereignty-inspired actions in places such as Alberta and Quebec. Despite the omnipresence of a rapidly changing, interconnected, and complex world that called for a governance defined by networks and subsidiarity (Goldsmith and Eggers 2004; Kettl 2002), the centralized mindset of the federal Liberal government has frozen the country into a simple either/or dilemma: choosing between central control and chaos.

This centralization of power has produced sporadic misuse of power by the federal Liberal government of the day, in a vain attempt to maintain central control. But such occasional misuses of power by the centre cannot legitimize permanently crippling the government of the day, nor can they legitimize creating a Manichean split between politics/policy and administration, and ignoring the central maven function of the clerk, and suggesting the quartering of this key function of coordination, thereby considerably weakening the Canadian system of governance.

Called for are

- a better understanding of the dynamics of governance in a world where power, resources, and information are ever more widely dispersed and where collaboration, networking, and social learning are crucial (Paquet 1999b);
- a questioning of the ideologies of centralization or chaos (indeed centralization at all costs) and of state-centricity (manifested in old-style Liberal politics) that have recently perverted the governance of the country;
- a search for ways to reduce the inevitably increasing disconcertation by means other than uniformity-generating centralization and coercion, including through a philosophy of subsidiarity and polycentric governance;

- a recognition of the aberrational circumstances that
  led to the sponsorship affair;
- a genuine exploration of the potentialities of a truly
  decentralized mode of governing the Canadian
  federation that might make the "abnormal times"
  of the 1990s an unlikely set of circumstances for the
  future; and
- an awareness of the need to preserve the capacity
  of the government of the day to govern, of the
  centrality of fail-safe mechanisms to fend off
  sabotage, and of creative maven work to ensure
  that reasonable and effective arrangements are
  continually negotiated.

None of these underpinnings of the sponsorship affair that
led to the mishaps (and to the Gomery inquiry) was probed
by the commission. It chose instead to focus on "proximate
sources" of the problem, on culpability, and on punishment.

WHAT GOMERY COULD HAVE DONE

Two broad areas call for particular attention.

The first one relates to the interface between policy/politics
and administration and the new forms of collaboration and
consultation required between politicians and bureaucrats,
all the while avoiding inappropriate political intrusions
in the operations of the state when they are not warranted;
the new horizontality and soft accountabilities demanded
in the relationships among groups of interested parties,
stakeholders, and levels of government in these interactions
in normal times; and the role of the clerk as a linchpin at the
core of the process of governing—a governing that is capable
of engineering important effective trade-offs, adjudication,
and compromises in difficult times and of providing fail-safe
mechanisms in truly abnormal times.

The second one pertains to the complex relationships among
the deputy minister, the responsible minister, and Parliament

and the blurring of these roles necessary for good governance, with the soft but intelligent accountabilities that ensue there. It also pertains to the need for great transparency and legitimacy in the whole system of selection of qualified officials, but with due concern for the complexity of the nexus of relationships within which the officials are nested, the need to ensure the appropriate degree of integration of differing perspectives, and the degree of trust needed for good governance.

In both areas, extreme caution is required.

THE POLICY/POLITICS–ADMINISTRATION INTERFACES

Policy refers broadly to patterns of action or inaction in the face of particular circumstances. Today federal state inaction may often be the best course of action since modern governance does not depend on the top-down dominium of the state but requires a high degree of collaboration among sectors (private, public, civic) and among levels of government. These interfaces are so complex that a good deal of ongoing and evolving interaction is essential, and social learning is a must. In the face of such evolving complexities, the state need not be the major player at all times, and public managers need to rely more and more on interpersonal and interorganizational processes as complements (and even at times as substitutes) for hierarchy and authority (Kettl 2002, 168).

All this need for nuance and flexibility cautions against the Gomery obsession with clear demarcations and robust firewalls. One should resist this kind of Manichean reform, which may go too far in trying to take politics out of operations and, in so doing, damage Canadian governance. There is a necessary continuous dialogue between politics/policy and administration that must not be artificially spooked. This dialogue constitutes the most important interface at the core of social learning and should not be stultified by firewalls or an urge to pinpoint responsibility at all times. Gomery's recommendations (if accepted holus-bolus) would paralyze the social-learning process by preventing the required and appropriate intervention of elected officials in the conduct of the public household.

The suggestion that the role of the clerk of the Privy Council should be fragmented may neutralize the power of the executive, but it would result in the governing system's losing one of its most important spaces for engineering important collaborative arrangements and effecting difficult trade-offs. At the interface of the political world, the executive world, and the bureaucratic world, the clerk is instrumental in effecting some of the crucial linkages in the governing apparatus and in helping the ship of state to navigate through the blurred world of politics/policy and administration. Without this integrative and syncretic locus of "power with," the ship of state would lose considerable effectiveness. A particularly deleterious impact on overall governance would ensue.

This does not mean, however, that the explicit role of the clerk cannot be or should not be refined or that specific clerks may not have failed in this important task. There may even be a need to rethink the role of the clerk, in light of the context in which it must operate these days, in order to enable the incumbent to play better the evolving roles of social architect and trade-off generator.

In particular, we would re-emphasize (1) the crucial complementarity of the three roles played by the clerk (deputy minister to the prime minister, secretary to cabinet, head of the public service), (2) the need to ensure that clerks neglect none of these functions (as some have been wont to do); and (3) the requirement to re-establish the central importance of the clerk as social architect and organizational designer over and beyond the necessity of the clerk's being a trade-off definer and a fixer (Hubbard and Paquet 2006a).

A crucial consequence of the need to live with a great deal of blurring of roles at these interfaces is the necessity to rely on *moral contracts* (Paquet 1992, 2005c, Chapters 4 and 6). These soft accountability arrangements are not at all akin to legitimizing "anything goes." They simply embody the flexibility and requisite subtlety for ensuring effective coordination in turbulent and changing times, when continuous adjustments are called for by groups pursuing different objectives but whose fate is inextricably interrelated. There has been little explicit use of moral contracts, but clearly they constitute an instrument that is well adapted to the need for flexible and evolving collaboration when effective formal arrangements are not possible and when the blurring of roles not only is inevitable but has also become a way of life.

In her Reith Lectures, Onora O'Neill has shown that real, intelligent accountability is built on trust and moral contracts and that "currently fashionable methods of accountability damage rather than repair trust" (2002, 77-78). Unfortunately, Gomery's report does not appear to point in that direction.

THE M-DM-P INTERFACES

The minister–deputy minister–Parliament (M-DM-P) inter-faces can also be improved, but the improvement should be carried out much more subtly than Gomery suggests. For instance, in his second report, Gomery wants deputy ministers and senior officials to be "accountable before" (but not "accountable to") the PAC in their own right for their statutory and delegated management responsibilities. This approach could be construed as radical but unobjectionable if it is assumed to have split hairs correctly, although some have argued that it amounts to "giving the public service a separate constitutional identity from the government" that "will 'impair' management and even undermine accountability" (May 2006b). But even if the more charitable interpretation is used, it should not end up being taken advantage of to drive a wedge between the minister and the deputy minister or lead to the minister's being unburdened of any responsibility or immunized from "real accountability." A more targeted approach, carrying less risk of hamstringing the legitimate ability of the government of the day to govern, would involve deputy ministers and senior officials answerable to ("accountable before") the PAC in their own right (as opposed to on behalf of their ministers) for the two kinds of specifics that seem to cover most of the problems raised by the sponsorship affair.

These specifics, for which they have been given responsibility under the Federal Accountability Act (FAA), would be (1) assurance that the management of resources allocated to their departments is *in compliance with* the relevant Treasury Board policies, regulations, standards, and periodic audits and (2) with respect to Section 34(1) of the FAA (the provision that requires them to certify that the work has been performed, the payment is according to contract, and the claim for payment is reasonable). This requirement would apply whether or not the resources entrusted to the deputy ministers resulted from their own statutory or delegated responsibilities. In every other respect, deputy ministers would continue to be answerable on behalf of their ministers, as they are today. And overall they would continue to be "accountable to" the government in all respects.

In the same spirit, one must be critical of Gomery II's pleas (1) for an open and competitive appointment process for selecting deputy ministers (similar to the one used in Alberta, which advertises and focuses on matching deputies to specific ministers), and (2) for boards of crown corporations (and not the governor in council) to select, appraise, and dismiss the CEOs of these corporations and (after the first round of appointments) to choose directors instead of the responsible minister. Both proposals have some serious drawbacks.

As Arthur Kroeger (2006) has suggested, the first one ignores the full role of the deputy minister, which is much broader than the departmental boundaries. It is not clear that the Alberta-like process would be able to ensure that all these other dimensions are appropriately taken into account.

As for the second one, the basic issue is whether or not there is (or remains) some public purpose for which a crown corporation of some sort is needed. If so, then there is a need for a link between the choice of its leadership and the government of the day. If not, then action should be taken to sell it or wind it up. Severing the leadership link, as Gomery II proposes, would seem to be either wrong-headed or solving the wrong problem.

In all these cases, transparency of the appointment process can no doubt be improved, as well as perceptions of reasonable accessibility by all those who have the ability to do the job, while still retaining the right of the prime minister to make the final recommendation to the governor in council. This process has already been experimented with in connection with the appointment of judges to the Supreme Court. Such a flexible and pragmatic approach would call for many variants applying to various groups of officials.

Better selection of officials may not suffice. There may also be a need for more sophistication in the definition of the officials' burdens of office and in the transparent evaluation of the ways in which they have carried out their mandates. One could also improve the sophistication and flexibility of the process of definition of officials' burdens of office immensely (and thereby their accountability) by making better use of explicit moral contracts.

An example is the letter that each deputy minister normally receives from the clerk on appointment to a new set of responsibilities. It could explicitly set out the deputy's duty *to be informed* about what is going on in the department *and to keep the clerk* (as the ultimate keeper of the bureaucratic safeguard of the public interest) *informed,* subject to the sanction of dismissal (Hubbard and Paquet 2005). An appropriate variation of this letter could also be used for administrative heads of other public sector entities, wherever that makes sense.

In the case of crown corporations, a parliamentary committee's periodic scrutiny of the mandate of the organization, and of the ways in which this mandate has been carried out (in light of both the formal statutes of the organization and the burden of office of its officials, as defined in their letters of appointment), if it were done well, would allow scope for both freedom of action and intelligent accountability of crown corporations.

While such arrangements are undoubtedly more complex than one might like, they match the degree of complexity of the tasks at hand. To insist upon slapping unduly simple procedures onto such complex duties can only lead to additional, complementary arrangements emerging in practice that will inevitably turn out to be less transparent and, as a result, more likely to generate unsatisfactory results.

SOME WORDS OF CAUTION
FOR THE PRIME MINISTER

The temptation for Prime Minister Stephen Harper to be seen as having quickly adopted many of the recommendations put forward by Gomery II has undoubtedly been high. Yet Harper's first reaction to Gomery II was wisely muted. Campaigning and governing are not quite the same process. The Conservative Party itself has come to realize that all desirable reforms are not necessarily as workable and realistic as they could or should be in an ideal world and that many seemingly desirable rules may have unfortunate unintended consequences. It will take some wisdom and courage for Prime Minister Harper to modify some of the recommendations put forward either in his electoral platform or in Gomery II (and indeed in the early version of the Federal Accountability Bill tabled in the House of Commons), and he will undoubtedly be chastised for it. Yet such modifications may be essential. If he is prudent, he may find some useful insights buried in the research studies that accompany Gomery II.

For instance, the emphasis on giving extended power to the ethics commissioner, the information commissioner, and the auditor general (built into the Conservative Party program) proceeds from the false assumption that on all these fronts more is better. But strengthening access to information and audit provisions may not necessarily be helpful. Alasdair Roberts (2006) points out that the existing provisions of the Access to Information Act seem to have driven a great deal of work underground. Benoit and Franks (2006) have also observed that the social-learning effect of the internal audit function has likely been hampered by the public availability of these studies.

And the idea of not allowing the prime minister to overrule the view of the ethics commissioner appears to undermine a fundamental democratic principle. It may make more sense to use the more pragmatic suggestion that comes from Pross's study for the commission (Gomery 2006, 2: 214): transparency might be sufficient to provide a good incentive. In other words, overruling the ethics commissioner in a particular case of conflict of interest would naturally form part of the public's judgment of the government of the day. The very existence of this possibility may well be enough to prevent overruling as a matter of course while allowing for such overruling in cases where the commissioner may have erred.

With regard to the open and competitive appointment process proposed for selecting the most senior administrative officials, it should be a question approached with great care. The Federal Accountability Act (FAA) proposed by the Conservative government is silent on the appointment of deputy ministers but turns to the Public Appointments Commission to "set merit-based requirements for appointments to government boards, commissions and agencies, to ensure that competitions for posts are widely publicized and fairly conducted" (FAA 2006, 5). This approach appears to be innocuous, but it may go too far in separating the government of the day from the leadership of its various administrative organizations.

One of the great dangers of the post–Gomery II era is the flurry of unreasonable and well-intentioned initiatives that it is likely to trigger that could generate deleterious unintended consequences in their pursuit of apparent absolute cleanliness. The public debate risks being cast in a fundamentalist either/ or mode, suggesting that Canada is faced with choosing between the status quo and embracing rational "perfection" when a middle-of-the-road pragmatic solution might in fact be highly desirable.

A better way of imagining the choices in a complex, messy, and evolving world is to avoid either extreme and to proceed carefully, doing minimal damage and then learning by doing (including the good and the bad unintended consequences) so that adjustments and refinements can be made as time goes on. Such approaches are usually savaged by ideologues, "solutionists," editorialists, and other grand tenors of the infotainment business as nothing but a lack of courage or vision. It is, however, often a sign of wisdom.

Pragmatism is not celebrated but is quite important, for often the best is an enemy of the good (Posner 2003). This means fending off the pressure from the sanctimonious to demand Gomery-like rules even when they are unreasonable. Bowing to them may generate unworkable governance arrangements from which it will be difficult to retreat.

In fact, Harper has already been called a liar by some purist, self-appointed ethical democracy watcher for having modified his planned Federal Accountability Act (Aubry 2006). Being deaf to such fundamentalist attacks may require the same wisdom that Ulysses displayed against the call of the sirens on his trip back from Troy: putting wax in his ears. But strategic deafness isn't good enough either.

Considerable public education is also required, for in many ways Gomery I and II have had the opposite impact from what was intended. Notwithstanding the best of intentions, they have misinformed and misled the public. By adopting an unduly narrow perspective, they have turned the issues into caricatures and set the stage for enormous pressure on governments to implement some simplistic, unreasonable, unworkable, and destructive governance arrangements. Debunking Gomery may be unpopular, but it may turn out to be a small step in a better direction for Canada.

CONCLUSION

Nevertheless, Gomery should not be completely written off. Some of the valid lessons and recommendations of Gomery II should not be lost. Separating the wheat from the chaff is the challenge—no matter that this is a daunting task in the field of public administration.

First, there is a serious, substantive barrier to public sector reform. As Francis Fukuyama puts it, the study of public management or public administration cannot be formalized not because of a lack of analytical rigour but "because of reasons inherent in the subject matter" (2004, 77). In public administration, rationality is limited, and organizations satisfice rather than optimize because actors are motivated not simply by narrow economic self-interest and technical rationality but also by norms of loyalty, reciprocity, tradition, and the like. The core idea is that "norms and cultural values serve as substitutes for formal monitoring-and-accountability systems" (79). Unsurprisingly, this calls for choosing more decentralized forms of organizations and a plurality of mixes of incentives, communication, exhortation, et cetera, according to circumstances.

In the public sector context, the importance and pervasiveness of norms mean that there is simply no optimal form of organization. Particular mixes of structures of incentives and normative environments call for different organizational forms. Organizational ambiguity prevails. This does not mean that anything goes: in sectors of high-specificity public sector output and low-volume transactions (e.g., central banking arrangements), changes may be effected by technocratic reform; in the case of low-specificity activities with high-volume transactions (e.g., law or education), especially in diverse societies subject to variance according to local conditions, not only is there no way for it to be fixed or solved by fiat, but also one may argue that there is a diversity of good solutions (Fukuyama 2004, 58, 84).

Second, there is a capacity barrier as well as one of will. This "black hole of public administration" (Fukuyama 2004, 43) has led experts, public intellectuals, and even institutions and organizations such as the Public Service Commission (before its wings were legislatively clipped) and the Association of Professional Executives of the Public Service of Canada (APEX) to avoid directly tackling the task of designing the social architecture of a refurbished governance system. The facts that such an architecture is essentially a contested notion, that there is no optimal organization, and that these institutions may have neither the capacity nor the legitimacy to overcome the distrust of other groups has led them to shy away from this terrain.

As a result, there is no place in Canada where the social architecture and design problems of the governance of the country are seriously and continuously examined, where the R&D required to continually reinvent new ways to adapt in order to ensure goodness of fit between circumstances and governance is perfected. This is why it is so difficult, when a special inquiry or commission comes up with a new blueprint, to elicit a meaningful critical response that is not simply inspired by romantic commitments to old designs or ideologies.

This is an area where public intellectuals have been glaringly absent and are badly needed (Paquet 2005b). Instead, indentured experts have occupied the terrain and have ensured that some of the sacred cows (a centralized federation, rigid demarcations between politics/policy and administration, etc.) are staunchly defended. It is crucial that a broader range of viewpoints be aired on these issues. Otherwise, there is much danger that the *à prendre ou à laisser* attitude will prevail and that pragmatic politicians defending *temperantia* and *prudentia* will be unduly chastised.

It is therefore important that debates about public management and governance involve all the producers of governance—not only professionals but also amateurs—so that public sector reforms can be shaped by those who have a vested interest in these processes and by those who are meant to be served by them. This need for inclusion calls for Gomery's suggestions to be much more widely and fully understood and discussed, so that citizen pressure can support them when they are reasonable but oppose them vigorously when they are likely to do more damage than good.

WHAT JUSTICE GOMERY FAILED TO SEE

[A] couple of loose ends needed tying.
—Jane Jacobs (1992)

INTRODUCTION

Taking a careful look at the Gomery proposals to repair the public governance apparatus before rushing into implementing them may be crucial but is hardly sufficient. One must also go beyond Justice Gomery's myopic analysis of proximate causes of the sponsorship saga and look at the dynamics that have been the root cause of the whole affair. This approach calls for a much broader contextual perspective and a richer appreciation of the forces at work and of the dysfunctions of the Canadian federal system.

As we mentioned earlier, blinkers prevented Gomery from exploring this broader context, and what he thereby failed to see made his inquiry immensely less relevant than it might have been and his recommendations consequently much less useful. To take a full measure of Gomery's failure to produce a report that would have gone beyond routine administrative repairs, one must become conscious of the fullness of the realities that Gomery failed or refused to see. His blinkered view prevented him from developing an appreciation of the sweeping change in the process of transforming the institutional order and of the seemingly determined efforts to oppose such changes by the Ottawa Liberal officialdom and its acolytes. Yet *there* lie the profound causes of the sponsorship saga.

The old, big-G institutional order has slowly been fading away in Canada for decades, and a new, small-g one has slowly and inexorably been taking its place. Increasingly in Canada, especially at the local level, people, groups, and organizations are getting together to invent their way out of urgent shared crises that cannot be ignored any longer. Governments remain involved, if and when they are needed, but citizens are increasingly critical of the price they have to pay in terms of responsiveness, timeliness, red tape, and bottom-line costs, if and when governments get involved.

Gomery's inquiry was in denial vis-à-vis this emerging order. As a result, his analyses and his recommendations did not take it into account, and this oversight has been costly. As a matter of consequence, (1) Gomery failed to factor in the dynamics of the new institutional order *en émergence*; (2) he did not grasp either the new complexities and dynamics of leadership in a world where nobody is in charge or the challenges for those whose power is rooted in the old order and are threatened by the emerging one; and (3) therefore, he was led to embrace both a most unrealistic vision of Canadian federalism and a deeply flawed model of Canadian public administration as foundations for his recommendations.

THE EMERGING STRATEGIC STATE REDUX

For the past two or three decades, the world has been swept up in tumultuous change. It has become less and less easy to pretend that big-G government was in charge; rather, a relatively more decentralized governance regime has emerged (see Table 6.1).

On the one hand, the inability of Western-style democracies such as Canada in adjusting to this new world and coping

Table 6.1: The Drift from G to g

	G → g Drift	
Key Characteristics	Public sector ≥* private sector (*perceived as more effective)	Private sector ≥* public sector (*perceived as more effective)
	Redistribution on the basis of rights	Redistribution on the basis of needs
	Soft egalitarianism	Subsidiarity
	Centralization	Decentralization

with the new challenges well has left the state vulnerable to a variety of criticisms. The brand of welfare state in good currency has been attacked on grounds that can be subsumed under a few headings (Duncan 1985; Paquet 1999a, 1999b).

1. *Overgovernment and government overload:* The state is presented as a kind of arthritic octopus, an inept leviathan unable, despite massive growth, to do much to meet the demands of the citizenry; as a result, it has triggered weakened citizen compliance, growing civic indifference, and much disillusionment (King 1975).
2. *A legitimation deficit:* The public has ceased to believe that the state has any moral authority or technical ability to deal with the issues at hand; this would explain the citizenry's disaffection and withdrawal of support (Habermas 1973).
3. *A fiscal crisis:* The state is unable to reconcile its dual obligation to attenuate social difficulties and to foster the process of capital accumulation without

generating fiscal deficits that in the long run are
unbearable (O'Connor 1973).

4. *Social limits to growth:* The three crucial dimensions
    of our social organization (liberal capitalism, mass
    democracy, and a very unequal distribution of both
    material and symbolic resources) cannot coexist
    easily—democratic egalitarianism (in society)
    generates compulsive centralism (in the polity) to
    redistribute more and more resources with little
    success in reducing inequality and greater success
    in shackling the productive capacity of the economic
    system (Hirsch 1976).

On the other hand, the emergence of this kind of (g) world
(in which nobody is in charge) has important implications
for any institutional order in an advanced democracy such as
Canada if it is going to be reasonably effective. First, there is a
growing yearning both on the left and on the right for a well-
defined code of moral obligations to underpin the realization
of a good society—a *public philosophy.* Second, there is a need
to stimulate and enable a reframing of views of the public
realm highlighting the need for *preceptoral politics.* Third,
resilience and learning may be the only competitive advantage
of countries and companies. Fourth, this leads to important
design principles for the social architecture of the public realm.
Fifth, there will be an increase in ill-structured or wicked
policy problems (where the goals are unclear and the means-
ends relationship is unclear), with *norm holding* as the best
possibility. And sixth, the state itself must become a *learning
organization.* Each of these implications has consequences for
the state and/or its political leaders if it and they are to be
effective to any significant degree.

PUBLIC PHILOSOPHY

Both on the left and on the right, there is a longing for people
at large (i.e., civil society) to provide a well-defined code of

moral obligations that can underpin the realization of the good society. However, the "built-in restraint[s] derived from morals, religion, custom, and education" considered by Adam Smith as a prerequisite before one could safely trust men (and women) to "their own self-interest without undue harm to the community" are no longer there (Hirsch 1976, 137). Marquand (2004) concurs.

The disappearance of this socio-cultural foundation has been noted and deplored, and much has been written about the need to rebuild it, but it has also become clear that it is futile to hope for some replacement for these values to come about by *immaculate conception* in civil society. As a result, many have called on the state and on political leaders to accept their responsibility as second-best moral agents (Mead 1986; Wolfe 1989). This could easily degenerate into a Hegelian-flavoured broth if the state ever came to be regarded as the fundamental societal organism with moral purposes that transcend those of individual citizens (Paquet 2005e). Such an outcome is not desirable. What must be allowed to emerge is a pluralist philosophy of the public realm that recognizes that there are many types of legitimate decision making and many sources of legitimate diversity (Galston 2002). This pluralist public philosophy must keep in check both the possibility of there being undue power of state institutions over all aspects of social life and the propensity to centralize power and deny the *droits à la différence*. Indeed, it must distill a vision, a sense of direction, and a commitment to ideals that encourage differentiation and subsidiarity. Such a public philosophy can be both *constraining* (in the sense that it echoes some fundamental choices and therefore excludes many possibilities) and *enabling* (in the sense that it provides a foundation on which a coherent pattern of institutions and decisions in the public realm can be built).

The recent squabbles about the recognition of les Québécois as a nation or a distinct society are quite revealing on this front: pluralism is gaining ground but only slowly and painfully.

PRECEPTORAL POLITICS

Enormously important in the emergence of this pluralist philosophy as well is what Charles Lindblom has labelled "preceptoral politics": formal and informal leaders from all sectors becoming educators, animateurs, people called upon to *reframe* views of the public realm, to design the organizations of mutual education, and to "set off the learning process" necessary to elicit, if possible, a latent consensus (Marquand 1988).

Such learning is unlikely to occur easily or well in today's deeply diverse society, either through national-level institutions or through institutions that lie completely or even primarily in the public sector. The institutions will likely have to be *middle-range* (*meso*) ones, possibly built upon what are emerging as new units of analysis for policy development, such as city-regions and communities of practice (Hubbard and Paquet 2005), or they will be networks designed to promote communication and cooperation on a scale of issues that mobilizes existing groups and communities in meso forums likely to mobilize the commitment of the citizenry in organizations when needed (Hubbard and Paquet 2006b).

RESILIENCE AND LEARNING

Faced with a turbulent environment, effective societal governance demands *resilience* and *learning*. As a result, it is here that the state can and should play a key role. It can help to nurture, support, and enable the necessary societal resilience and learning in a variety of ways, including becoming involved as a *broker,* as an *animateur,* and as a *partner* in participatory planning.

In complex, advanced capitalist socio-economies like Canada's, the bottom line is that the state can play new central mediating roles that go well beyond mechanical interventions but that are far from paternalistic "ruling" and that go beyond the housekeeping roles and offsetting functions of the past that required minimal input from the citizenry. To do this, the state must bet on a flexible exercising of control and on organizational learning for itself that is extremely effective. Its new triple role—providing (and enabling) mediating structures, setting patterns for the provision of services, and helping to educate individuals in their mutual and civil commitments—requires revitalization to match these new demands (Etzioni 1983).

But the fluid and seemingly scattered system of governance in the postmodern strategic state that it implies must be anchored in a clear sense of direction in order to underpin the state's strategic actions. So there must be a *plan*. Most state leaders in advanced socio-economies outside North America have such a plan, a direction for strategic intervention, and a public philosophy that will articulate and rationalize it; "they do not publish their plan because it would never gain consent. Yet it is not what one ought to call a conspiracy. ... The plan is not entirely conscious or systematic, and it cannot be as long as it is not written, published, debated, revised and so on. But it is not what you could call a secret" (Lowi 1975, 116).

This plan serves as a gyroscope for the state in the definition of actions taken by its personnel, serving as the basis for a *double-looped learning process* in them, as organizational learning demands (i.e., not only finding a better means of learning to do what is done better but also, and more importantly, finding the right goals and learning whether the objectives being pursued are the right ones) (Argyris and Schön 1974). But such learning by the state cannot be done by elected officials alone. It can be achieved only when a *public philosophy, appropriately defined,* can provide the framework *within and with which* the executive and its bureaucratic and political advisers can operate. Elected officials and bureaucrats must work symbiotically, with ever more devolution of discretion to bureaucrats and to local officials.

DESIGN PRINCIPLES

For a social architecture of the public sector that enables the required societal resilience and social learning, the design principles are clear. The first is the principle of *subsidiarity*, according to which "power should devolve on the lowest, most local level at which decisions can reasonably be made, with the function of the larger unit being to support and assist the local body in carrying out its tasks" (Bellah et al. 1991, 135-136). It is built on the centrality of the autonomy of active citizens who have to take primary responsibility for their own welfare and the welfare of their families. Beyond the duty to nurture, support, and enable this centrality of active citizens (which itself needs to be governed by subsidiarity among and within governments), the authority of governments is to intervene based not on any rights or entitlements ordained from above but primarily from the citizens' need for help. Thus, in these instances, governments act in a subsidiary way as the guarantor and enabler of choice in public goods, usually in the same way as a reserve army intervenes in case of need. It also calls for policy choices and delivery designs and decisions to be made at the lowest, most local, reasonable level (starting with the citizen).

The rationale for this principle is that the institutions closer to the citizen are those likely to be the closest approximation to organic institutions—that is, to institutions that are likely to emerge *undesigned* from the sheer pressure of well-articulated needs and likely to require minimal yearly redesigning. In special circumstances, the highest order of government may of course have to take the lead when it is best placed to do so (e.g., in dealing with external threats to the society, such as terrorism or epidemiological crises).

Such an approach does not mean the death of central government but the demise of big government as the morphological assurance of societal resilience. When the ground is in motion, the bulkier and the more centralized the government, the more it will flounder. The lean new central strategic state must deal with norms, standards, and general directions. The process of ministering to the public, and delivering a service well adapted to its needs, must be devolved to the local level. Such a government would provide services (directly, indirectly, or both) within a framework agreed to nationally or regionally.

The second design principle is that of ensuring the requisite amount of *organizational learning* by the public sector so that the necessary real co-evolution and effective cooperation of the public sector with the other two sectors can materialize (Goldsmith and Eggers 2004). Such social learning entails an *effective citizen-based evaluation feedback* to ensure that the services produced, financed, or regulated by the public realm meet with the required standards of efficiency, economy, and effectiveness and are consonant with the spirit of the agreed standards or norms. This is a central cybernetic loop feature in the refurbished state. It is essential if organizational learning is to proceed as quickly as possible (Crozier 1987).

NORM HOLDING

Since policy makers in the strategic state face more and more ill-structured or *wicked* problems (where the goals are unclear and the means-ends relationships are uncertain), elected officials and bureaucrats are going to be ill equipped to manage in the usual hierarchical strict goal-setting and control mode (Rittel and Webber 1973). The best that one can hope for with problems like these is some *norm holding* (Vickers 1965).

This approach underpins a process of policy making based on intelligence and innovation within issue domains: a dynamic monitoring by those closer to the issues, which feeds an innovative learning process and embraces all stakeholders. But this new form of public management, based on continuing feedback and constant problem reformulation as experiences accumulate, requires new partnerships between the public, private, and social realms, between elected officials, bureaucrats, and players from other sectors, et cetera. This is a world of moral contracts among members of networks.

These negotiated norms are much less rigid and less likely to foster adversarial relations than if the work is done through formal regulations and rules. "The general idea is that if it is possible to agree on the broad principles that particular sets of regulations strive to achieve, it should be possible to produce a flexible set of arrangements that satisfy the interested parties without hamstringing operations" (Morgan 1988, 163).

LEARNING ORGANIZATION

Finally, if the state is to become *a learning organization,* as it must, ensuring a constant dialogue with the citizenry and improving the communicational competence of its citizens are going to require some organizational development and institutional building: one cannot rely exclusively on organic feedback. New instrumentalities are necessary if a capacity to learn at the centre (from the citizen and from the agency delivering the service) *and* a capacity for quick feedback and instantaneous action are to materialize when governments do not appear to do the right thing.

LEADERSHIP IN A WORLD
WHERE NOBODY IS IN CHARGE

In today's world, built on a multiplicity of flexible arrangements, governing by network is the rule, and effective leadership might best be described in Harlan Cleveland's words as "bringing people together to make something different happen" (2002, xv). This cannot be brought about top down by coercion but mostly by means of negotiated agreements. For this sort of leadership of equals to work, rich communications, coordinating activities, relation building, and trust are required.

In today's world of collaboration, much depends on how people work together and how they communicate. Leaders are truly connectors who instruct members of their communities of practice in a light way, often by example. This approach transforms the usual pattern of motivation: one can no longer be satisfied with monetary carrots and accountability sticks. Trust and professionalism are crucial when collaboration is central (Evans and Wolf 2005).

Public sector leaders must maximize public value by concentrating on building on core government capabilities and identifying which partners the state might benefit most from collaboration with and in which ways. The public sector becomes itself a connector and an enabler and not necessarily a doer. This does not entail neglect of the public interest in any way. The necessary governing by network does, however, wield a different sort of power: *power with* instead of *power over.*

What is necessary for an organization or institution or a socio-economy to be led effectively might succinctly be referred to as public spaces and conductivity. Public spaces are places where the necessary conversations and communications can occur. It has been shown that in the process of product development both that such conversational spaces are a fascinating locus of innovation and creativity and that their absence may inhibit growth (Lester and Piore 2004). In the same manner, the lack of a public space where the different stakeholders might be able to "work things out" is a frequent source of governance failure (Hubbard and Paquet 2006b).

Conductivity refers to the capability to effectively transmit high-quality knowledge throughout the organization as well as with and between citizens and employees (Saint-Onge and Armstrong 2004, 19). Such high conductivity, likely to make organizations more effective, is shown to depend on a strong alignment of its capabilities (strategy, culture, structure, and system). Leadership in this context is geared to assuring the alignment of these different components as well as the alignment of the frames of reference of the different stakeholders.

While it is possible to work on all these fronts to effect the required alignment, it is easier to work on systems: that is, "the assembly of all horizontal and vertical processes across the organization that enable it to implement its strategy" (Saint-Onge and Armstrong 2004, 155). This is not necessarily the only way to proceed, but betting on systems change (like betting on mechanisms) appears to be promising because it represents an easier way to intervene than using the more direct approach. Governing indirectly and through networks, negotiations, and contracts may seem to be ineffective, but when collaborative governance is *de rigueur* the time spent upfront in negotiations generates a great deal of effectiveness at the implementation phase later on.

These alignments are complex in the case of the Canadian state. The public sector in Canada is a four-dimensional world comprising

- many levels of government (federal, provincial, regional, local);
- a mix of private (quid pro quo), public (coercion), and social (reciprocity) mechanisms;
- different types of public servants: super-bureaucrats, guardians, professionals, and more broadly, employees; and
- various sorts of arrangements, ranging from political deals, to rules shaping the bargains between politicians and bureaucrats, to routine administrative activities, to regime-type loose forms of moral contracts.

At any one time, the natural tensions in the public sector translate into a crystallization of the state that involves all these dimensions.

This precarious "social armistice" may be a stable equilibrium, but it is always a fragile and temporary one. While it does not completely transform itself overnight, some institution or practice—however small—that plays a part in this armistice evolves every day, possibly unnoticed.

Our conjecture is that the tensions in the public sector today, and for the foreseeable future, will tend to get the state to crystallize (1) with its centre of gravity closer to the local level than before, (2) with a smaller but robust government sector, (3) with a smaller core public service, and (4) with a larger portion of arrangements that are much less formalized, or being led in the political realm, and much more informal and embodied in conventions.

Each of these four shifts has implications for the structure and functioning of the public sector:

- more collaboration needed between levels of government;
- reinforcement of local governance;
- reduction in the size of the public sector;
- more use of networks among and within governments and with players in other sectors (i.e., more associative governance);
- a smaller core public service;
- more use of moral (as opposed to formal or legal) contracts;
- more choice for citizens in service delivery of public goods; and
- less use of coercion.

This sort of "soft voice and low key" leadership of the state does not mean that the role of the state has been trivialized. The strategic state clearly has a reduced scope in comparison to the welfare state, but this does not mean that state capacity is necessarily reduced as a result (Fukuyama 2004) or that the state cannot exercise this strength in powerful if soft ways. The role of *animateur* or *entremetteur* does not mean that its influence or capacity to intervene needs to be impoverished or weakened in any way. But it does mean that its leadership will of necessity be different than it has been for a long time.

CANADIAN PUBLIC ADMINISTRATION

The shifting role of the state obviously calls for changes in the nature of Canadian public administration. This shift has occurred with much resistance from those who saw the new decentralization as threatening their power base and authority. Indeed, this resistance has led to a strong defensive rationalization of the status quo and a celebration of the existing "Canadian public administration model" (Gow 2004), which is presented as a source of national pride and potential export and has received the imprimatur of the Canada School of Public Service. It is not surprising that Justice Gomery chose to embrace such a view. This *image d'Épinal* contrasts greatly with the perspective that has emerged from the analyses of the earlier chapters and with what is really going on in Canada.

GOW'S "CANADIAN MODEL?"

In describing the Canadian model, Gow (2004) seems to proceed very carefully. He even adds a question mark after the title to indicate the tentative nature of his effort to capture the spirit of Canadian public administration as it now operates. But this formal prudence does not hide the fact that his presentation is deeply rooted in strongly held ideological presumptions: a state-centric worldview; a staunch defence of the main elements of the traditional welfare state, with its foundational egalitarianism, centralization, and somewhat priestly view of public servants as a lump of guardian-knights; and a great suspicion of any new design principles. Gow chooses to define subsidiarity in a whimsical if revealing way as something "which seems to mean 'look after yourself'" (10), and he has openly expressed hope that the Canadian model he has imagined "will remain basically intact" (22). A side-by-side comparison of Gow's model with what appears to emerge from a more dispassionate look at the present scene is contained in Table 6.2.

**Table 6.2: Canadian Public Administration:
Two Perspectives**

	Gow's Model	The Strategic State
I N A D E Q U A T E	*Homogeneous* (hierarchical) *governance* mode: —protected state core —federal government dominance	*Heterogeneous* (different forms of integration and institutional *métissage*) *co-governance* mode: —state as *animateur*, catalyst, enabler, failsafe —subsidiarity
	Public sector as a *whole* —equivalent to political sphere	Public sector as three intermingling, overlapping *zones* —politics, "stateness," regimes
	Professional public service as *one lump of labour*	Professional public service as *four types of labour* (super-bureaucrats, guardians, professionals, employees)
I N A C C U R A T E	Striking Characteristics	Today's Reality
	Strong political (federal) *control* (aggravated by Liberal domination)	*Control* increasingly *challenged by others* —work arounds (Internet drug sales to US) —provincial defiance (Kyoto, Gun Registry) —turning away (voter turnout decline)
	Strong legal framework buttressed by *Charter*	Rule of law paramount but *growing* —instability (AG media overstatements) —unpredictability (Supreme Court on health care) —volatility (more Charter-based challenges)

(continued)

	Autonomous, non-partisan professional public service	*No longer autonomous or non-partisan* —government, deputy heads have most key HR levers despite technicalities —major union intervention in election campaign in 1980s
	Pragmatism and moderation	*True of citizens but not so true of* —politicians (climate of blaming, inability to really change, few incentives for experimentation)—professional public service (institutional aversion to real change)
	Tolerance for *ambiguity*	*True of citizens but not so true of* —politicians (evade, avoid, misrepresent) —senior officials (at best silent acquiescence)
W O R L D V I E W	State-centric	Non-state-centric

GOW'S "CANADIAN MODEL" AS INACCURATE

Gow (2004) describes the five "most striking characteristics" of his Canadian model—the potential for strong political control, a strong legal framework, an autonomous, non-partisan professional public service, a tradition of pragmatism and moderation, and a fairly strong tolerance for ambiguity— and he explains each. In fact, when compared with reality, these characteristics turn out to be overstatements to varying degrees.

> ... The potential for strong political control [original italics removed]. This characteristic has been present all along, but is aggravated by the recent domination of one party, the Liberals, the weak opposition and lack of experience of the members of the elected legislature. The principal restraints are federalism, the Charter, parliamentary agents and public opinion. (21)

The presumption is that strong political *federal* control is an asset in Canada's federal system, yet it is seen as "aggravated" by the recent Liberal domination. One might reasonably suggest that this sort of control may have been a feature of the old big-G model but that it stands in the way of implementing effective small-g regimes. Indeed, such strong federal control appears to stand in the way of the improved intergovernmental collaboration required today. The Gow model assumes that federal, top-down state control is part of the Canadian way and implies that any form of governance that is not state-centric and federally controlled à la Trudeau will be dysfunctional.

> ... A strong legal framework [original italics removed], buttressed by the Charter and the courts and, to some extent, by independent control agencies. (21)

The rule of law prevails in Canada, and this is an important basis for sustainable democracy. But many of the agencies and super-bureaucrats mentioned above have been heavily criticized in recent times. We have noted the temptation of the Office of the Auditor General to overstate serious messages. We have also noted misuse of the charter by the Supreme Court of Canada to transform "wishes" into "entitlements" that are caricatured as "rights" (Leishman 2006). This sort of buttressing has generated much puzzlement. In the light of recent experience, failing to entertain the possibility that the role of the super-bureaucrats and the uppermost senior officials might be in need of redefinition or review is overcome by cognitive dissonance.

> At its heart, there is an autonomous, non-partisan, professional public service [original italics removed] that has proven itself willing and able to work with governments of different parties and of differing ideological tendencies. The present thrust of the leadership of this public service is to install a "learning organization" as a way to ensure its survival and its best contribution. (21)

The federal public service has proven itself willing and able to work with governments with different ideological bents. Nevertheless, the reality is that the federal public service is no longer either autonomous or non-partisan. The same is true in most if not all of the provinces and territories.

The 2003 Public Service Modernization Act put most managerial levers for the human resource management of the federal public service into the hands of ministers or, in a few cases, the deputy heads (many of whom serve at pleasure and all of whom depend upon the prime minister's recommendation for appointment or reappointment). As a result, it is hard to argue that the public service is autonomous, even if, technically, the independent Public Service Commission controls staffing (Hubbard 2004). It is also hard to assert that the public service has been non-partisan since the time, in the mid-1980s, when one of its biggest unions openly campaigned against a political party that ran on a platform implying a reduction in the size of the public service.

And while most federal deputy ministers are appointed from within the ranks of the professional public service, the same is not true of most of their provincial/territorial counterparts. In these cases, ideological alignment with the executive is considered to be essential.

> Our public service and its political leaders have a tradition of pragmatism and moderation [original italics removed] that keeps it evolving. We have mildly embraced downsizing and the new public management but kept politics in the picture and avoided over committing to one or two radical reforms. (21)

Canadians are pragmatic and moderate, but it is quite another thing to presume that their leaders and public servants are like most Canadians in this regard. In fact, public service leaders have become more self-serving and have become resistant to change and quite defensive as a result of it. This is often the rationale for what Gow has kindly called a mild embrace of downsizing and reform.

Political leaders often act as if they are obsessed with blaming, not learning, and political correctness has become a soft form of despotism. As a result, the federal administrative apparatus appears to be unwilling and/or unable to change and to lack any incentive to experiment with better approaches. Pragmatism and moderation appear here to be synonymous with lethargy and dynamic conservatism.

> ... features fairly strong tolerance for ambiguity [original italics removed] as represented by multi-layered government and multiple loyalty of many of its citizens. At present, new forms of government for the northern territories and self government agreements with various aboriginal communities reinforce this trend. (21)

Unfortunately, the real tolerance for ambiguity is low. In a world where politicians and the upper echelon of bureaucrats have been marshalling arguments about the need for "clarity" at all costs, and where ministers and senior bureaucrats have declared vertical fiscal imbalance a "logical impossibility," dogmas and theological arguments appear to be the law of the day in Ottawa—and the same fundamentalism/*intégrisme* appears to infect many provincial and territorial administrative systems.

The inadequacy of the Canadian model seemingly embraced by Gow can be gauged by its inability to respond to some of the fundamental questions raised earlier.

- It presumes that the present division of labour among politicians, state apparatus, and regimes is ideal and can be smoothly modified, when in fact most of the change happens by accident or chance or because of crises. The best examples of this are the complete paralysis of health care reforms and the dominance of ideology in a debate that prevents a major restructuring of the health care sector.
- It presumes that there is no need for a fundamental rethinking of Canadian public administration and perpetuates the myth that all federal public servants are guardians (in the sense of Jane Jacobs) and endowed with a *grâce d'état certaine*.

CONCLUSION

The compounding of a refusal to acknowledge the emerging institutional order, a denial of the need for new decentralized and softer modes of leadership, and the reprehensible complaisance in regarding the imaginary Canadian public administration à la Gow as quasi-perfect can only lead one not to take action.

Gow, like Dr. Pangloss, appears simply to assume that "tout est pour le mieux dans le meilleur des mondes" and that the fantasized mix of strong political control, buttressed by a strong legal framework and helped assiduously by a professional and autonomous public service, will generate all the requisite social learning through pragmatism, moderation, and tolerance for ambiguity. Consequently, Gow sees no need for concern and thus for change.

Justice Gomery appears to share this angelic view. For Gomery, as for Gow, a few flats and sharps suffice—if they are even necessary.

CONCLUSION

I'm simply referring to the obvious discrepancy between
your intention and the final outcome.
                                        —William Leiss (2006)

The thawing of the ethos that one is sensing may not be
as dramatic a transformation as the sort of true *perestroika*
that some are calling for, but maybe this is the only sort of
transformation that Canadians are willing to envisage or are
even capable of—a polite revolution (Ibbitson 2005).

How Canada will steer itself in today's interconnected,
fast-paced world is a question to which there is no simple
response on which most can agree. It will depend on the
constraints and damage inherited from the past, on Canada's
capacity to shed the shackles of state-centricity, on Canadians'
will and creativity to generate innovative ways to collaborate,
and on the acceptability of partitioning problems into issue
domains where meso-forums will make possible the genuine
experimentations and deliberations that are likely to result in
fruitful reforms agreeable to meaningful stakeholders.

The burden of the past is not inconsequential. The
difficulties experienced by Canadian federalism in coping
with the challenges of the new turbulent environment can be
ascribed to a great extent to a hyper-centralization syndrome
that had its roots in the post-1972 Trudeau years and that

was dangerously exacerbated by Trudeau's personal need to intervene publicly against the Meech Lake Accord in order to "lay hands on his victory over the provinces, celebrated with royal blessing on national television in 1982, and Brian Mulroney, for whom he had a contempt only equaled by that he had for Robert Bourassa" (Robertson 2001, 341), regardless of the cost to the country.

Although Gordon Robertson also argues that Clyde Wells should rightly bear "a large part of the blame" for the failure of the Meech Lake Accord, which had been accepted by all eleven governments, this last of the mandarins and former secretary to cabinet for federal/provincial relations points out tellingly in *Memoirs of a Very Civil Servant* the price that Canadian federalism has paid for one man's vanity. Robertson observes that

> we have never since 1990 been so close to an agreement that would have opened the way to negotiation on other national problems that are insoluble except by constitutional change: reform of the Senate, to meet the perennial western grievance, and the unfinished business of the aboriginals. Nothing in the Meech Lake Accord could have done the damage to Canada that has been done by its defeat—damage that is not ended. (2001, 348)

It is not our purpose in this conclusion to spell out in detail the way in which Canadian federalism should be reframed, restructured, and retooled to bolster the new institutional order and to ensure a genuine *perestroika* that would eliminate the sort of pressures that led to the sponsorship affair. This is a matter that would require more extensive discussions than are possible here. Our aim is to remind the reader of the root causes of the problems of present-day Canadian federalism, to sketch the broad outlines of the various scenarios that appear to be plausible at this time, and to identify the sort of organizational and cultural changes that will be necessary if a genuine *perestroika* is to become not only possible but also probable.

FOUR SCENARIOS

The federal Liberal Party (from Trudeau post-1972 on) has done everything it could to maintain the federal domination of the state and has done so in a confrontational and essentially destructive way. The Trudeau-Chrétien era was marked by personal autocracy, contempt for provincial and local authorities as well as for Parliament, and many manipulative activities to deceive a population regarded as fundamentally indentured to the Liberal Party for its guidance. It was done at first in an intellectually dismissive way that was not always detected and certainly not robustly opposed in the 1970s, when these manoeuvres were so easily swamped by the crises of the times (oil crisis, stagflation, deficit and debt, etc.).

By the time the Mulroney interregnum was over in 1993, the federal Liberal Party showed signs of becoming arrogantly and crassly autocratic: Jean Chrétien would say, in effect, that the only alternative to state-centricity and hyper-centralization Liberal Party–style was chaos. As a result, completely seduced by its own rhetoric, the federal Liberal Party felt compelled to "do something" (e.g., massive social marketing for the preservation of the old order, among other things) when the danger of what it saw as "balkanization" loomed large.

By the 1990s, it had become obvious that no one could claim to have all the information, resources, and power to steer the Canadian system, but the federal Liberal Party appears to have remained in denial. In the latter part of his tenure, Chrétien even allowed himself to comment in public that his whims could still rule the day. In the debates preceding the Social Union Agreement, he sounded like Louis XIV when he mused in public that sometimes on Monday he felt like giving the provinces more money, but then on Tuesday he did not (Paquet 1999b).

Even though there has been some evolution from big-G to small-g in the recent past, and a tendency for more private-public collaboration and intergovernmental cooperation, the federal Liberal Party has not relinquished its state-centric focus or its insistence on the necessity of maintaining robust control of the federation. The so-called pseudo-networked federalism scenario has received a good deal of support in the less dogmatic ranks of the federal Liberal Party. Collaboration has been seen as more necessary in the socio-political sphere to take into account the growing blurring of boundaries (especially between sectors and within and between levels of government) in an increasingly interdependent world. Still, most discussions of this new form of stewardship (once they are cleansed of their obfuscating rhetoric) appear to be driven to the conclusion that there is no hope of any such regime surviving unless the buck can be said to stop somewhere, unless ultimately someone is in charge (i.e., unless the central state continues to occupy the centre of the stage and to make final decisions even in normal times).

Of course, the federal Liberal Party had always assumed that in abnormal or crisis times, some extraordinary state control might/should be invoked, in the same manner that the War Measures Act may be invoked in crisis times. The mindset of the party appears to suggest a permanent state of extraordinary state control—*un état d'exception permanent* (Agamben 2003).

The big-G to small-g drift has shaped a scenario of "softer paternalism" in some more enlightened countries (*The Economist* 2006), but in Canada top-down autocratic and centralized decision making appears to have remained in force. Canada's approach remains fundamentally Hegelian: the state (always spelled with a capital S) is regarded as the fundamental societal "organism," with moral purposes that transcend those of its individual citizens, and it is assumed dogmatically that the state knows best.

Thus, the pseudo-networked scenario is quite tempting for the federal Liberal Party as a second-best option to the pure version of the "old order" in which it was firmly in charge. It is also tantalizing for the left-leaning phalanxes in general: warmly extending the offer to collaborate but only as long as the federal state remains hyper-centralized and in charge, because without such centralization ensuring that the loot is brought to the centre there cannot be the massive redistribution that is the central concern of the egalitarian left.

The lower portion of Figure C.1 opens the possibility of escaping from the Hegelian trap to some extent. It emphasizes the possibility of reducing state centricity by allowing individuals and/or lower-order governments to take a greater role.

The scenario connoted by the bottom left-hand quadrant—labelled separate facilities—combines the idea that no one is in charge with an emphasis on low collaboration. It builds on a "good fences make good neighbours" philosophy. The different levels of government and the different sectors (private, public, and social) would stick to their legitimate knitting, with as little trespassing as possible. While this may look like the continuation and expansion of today's silos, this scenario acknowledges, at the least, that no one is completely and fully in charge. It counts on sheer competition to provide the requisite coherence and harmonization.

The bottom right-hand quadrant scenario puts the emphasis on non-state-centric collaboration. It is built on the premise that one does not need credentialed stewards (e.g., politicians and bureaucrats) in charge to generate collaboration. Wikipedia, Linux, and VISA have clearly shown that coordination can emerge in other ways (Paquet 2005d). In this scenario, Canadian federalism is "open-source federalism": the state no longer occupies centre stage, and the people's will and ability to shape their own destiny are the main driver. In this last scenario, as in other open-source experiments, prototyping and serious play are of central importance (Schrage 2000), and in this regime, geared to promote growth, productivity, and innovation, the state would focus on the removal of the major sources of "unfreedoms" (Sen 1999).

Open-source federalism would entail a significant amount of experimentation and the acceptance that experiments will differ from sector/region to sector/region and will often fail. The guidepost in such experimentation, therefore, cannot be instant success but minimum regret. Governance and stewardship failures cannot be corrected by simply adding on mechanical contraptions. In the end, some reframing and some cultural change will be required.

We believe that this last scenario, while risky, is the most interesting one. Key to evolution in this direction is (1) a drift toward a form of federalism that, to the greatest extent possible, enables each citizen and group of citizens to have access to the "code" and to tinker freely with the way that the stewardship system works within certain well-accepted constraints, and (2) a priority given to "serious play" (i.e., the development of a premium on innovation and experimentation with the view that if experimentation is encouraged, necessary retooling, restructuring, and reframing are more likely to occur innovatively and productively). The state would remain the backstop in extraordinary circumstances (Paquet 2006b).

Figure C.1: Four Scenarios of Canadian Federalism

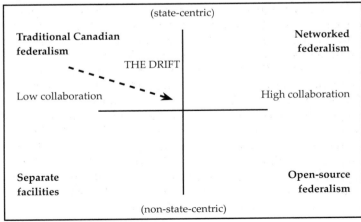

A BLESSING IN DISGUISE?

The Gomery reports chose to avoid this broad perspective, even though this is the locus and the root source of the difficulties that triggered the sponsorship affair: the new dynamic of governance in a world where power, resources, and information are widely distributed, with its philosophy of subsidiarity versus the counterideology of centralization-or-chaos. This is the basic conflict underpinning the sponsorship affair. What looked like the federal Liberal Party's dirty tricks was simply a way to maintain the stewardship of the Canadian socio-technical system in the upper reaches of Figure C.1.

The Martin government, anxious to appear to be on the side of the angels, forgot to keep a level head and reacted to the ongoing exposé of the Gomery inquiry by piling on reams of central rules under the crusading leadership of Reg Alcock at the Secretariat of the Treasury Board. This response drove a former secretary of the Treasury Board, as well as a former deputy minister, to publicly bemoan government-wide application of idealized management frameworks—what they called "the law of mandated utopias," which they believed are likely to jeopardize necessary management reform (Clark and Swain 2005).

Notwithstanding all these unfortunate unintended consequences of the Gomery road show, the Gomery inquiry *in toto* had some positive effects. First, it helped to create a climate of change in Canada, even if it deflected attention away from the deeper problems of the federation. Canadians slowly and hesitatingly became psychologically prepared to take a chance on a change of government. Second, it provided the Harper government—once elected on a decentralization platform—with a lever (i.e., "standing up for accountability") to start making progress on fundamental reforms.

But a number of wildcards were dealt and are therefore in play. On the one hand, the Harper government has stated clearly that "making the federation work better" is a priority and, to this end, has taken early action (e.g., loosening the federal grip on international representation, setting out principles for a new approach to restoring the fiscal balance, recognizing the reality of a Québécois nation). As a result, Canadians have slowly realized that the sky will not fall with a more pluralistic approach and with changes to the rigid administrative system that move it further away from the classical Westminster model. On the other hand, resistance to the transformations envisaged may be expected from within the world of politicians and bureaucrats.

First, it is not clear that "open-source federalism" will appeal to provinces and territories that have built their discourse on "acquired rights" rather than on innovation and experimentation. Second, the Liberal pundits in the media have already begun systematically to attack decentralization and to celebrate state-centricity in a manner that reveals the depth of intellectual programming and the resilience of the mindset that have resulted from sixty years of welfare statism. Third, there is already evidence of some concerted efforts by a fifth column in the uppermost rank of the federal bureaucracy to encapsulate and control efforts to effect a real reallocation of power to the provinces and localities or to open the federal game to experimentation and serious play.

PREREQUISITES TO A GENUINE *PERESTROIKA*

Any major transformation of the institutional order involves changes at three levels. First, the transformation must be apprehended as a legitimate idea that receives explicit or latent support (or at least no violent opposition) from the many powerful groups in the present order. Second, it has to translate into a variety of structural modifications of the traditional order, with consequent modification of roles and responsibilities. And third, it must crystallize into new rules of the game and new socio-technical arrangements. Theory (what business the organization is in), structures (roles and responsibilities), and technology (rules of the game) are intricately intertwined: any change in one has an impact on the others (Schon 1971).

Logically, one would prefer to move forward in three stages: change the theory, modify the structure, and tinker with the technology. However, organizational culture and the whole philosophy embodied in an institutional order are very difficult to transform. They are rooted in values and quite resistant to change. It is much easier to indulge in some tweaking of the structure and technology to tilt the system out of balance and thereby generate more fundamental changes. Yet often attempts to modify simple rules or techniques serve as lightning rods to mobilize citizens in uncanny ways. A few years ago the simple request that dog owners keep their animals on leashes on the public lands of the National Capital Commission (NCC) in Ottawa led to unforeseen calls to arms against the NCC. So there is no recipe for institutional change, and one can easily understand why Albert Hirschman suggests that when dealing with change, citizens should "modestly respect its unpredictability," for "change can only happen as a result of surprise, otherwise it could not occur at all, for it would be suppressed by the forces that are in favour of the status quo" (1995, 136). The Québécois nation debates of late 2006 are a case in point: change by surprise move. So it is with some circumspection that we venture to suggest two sets of prerequisites if a *perestroika* is to materialize.

The first set of prerequisites has to do with getting rid of the mental prisons, inherited from the past, that underpin the present overcentralized institutional order. These constraints are not necessarily well understood, but they are deeply anchored in the Canadian soul. So it is still perilous to challenge them and very difficult to uproot them.

REFORMING THE WESTMINSTER SYSTEM
The maxims of Westminster-style government are simple: separation of the bureaucracy in status from elected politicians,

final authority of ministers in office over the actions of officials, and lines of accountability running directly from officials to ministers to cabinet to Parliament. The Canadian federation is a non-interlocking set of at least eleven such systems—one for each of the two senior orders of government.

While this is an arcane subject, and most citizens would be unable to define the intricacies of the Westminster system, it has remained a robust feature in the mindsets of politicians and bureaucrats alike and a constant reference point. In a world in which boundaries are becoming blurred, roles are becoming fuzzier, and greater collaboration is called for, these maxims cannot be sustained, yet, as the Gomery reports show, tradition trumps rationality on this front.

New forms of cooperation between politicians and bureaucrats, but also between levels of government, have de facto evolved over time, and new ones will have to materialize. Moreover, it is unthinkable to continue to ignore the centrality of the dozen or so major cities in the country that are the true source of wealth of the nation and to treat them as mere creatures of the provinces. The new order will be characterized by fuzziness.

Constitutional amendments may not be a workable route to effect such changes. It is more likely that innovative administrative arrangements and declaratory pronounce-ments will be the most useful instruments. But these innovations will require both a new spirit of collaboration (with an end to parties taking refuge in constitutional wrangles to avoid accepting reasonable administrative arrangements) and the acceptance of soft, intelligent accountability in lieu of the rigid accountability framework implied by the Westminster regime.

SOFTENING THE EGALITARIAN IDEOLOGY
The second pillar of the old order is the egalitarian ideology that is so often used to bolster the requirement of hyper-centralization. It is argued that one could not proceed with the

required redistribution without the possibility of bringing a sufficient amount of fiscal resources to the centre. While there has been a slow and painfully resisted shift from strong to weak egalitarianism over the past few decades, egalitarianism remains a powerful ideology that has prevented efforts to decentralize government. There is a need for a decisive attack on this front and for a change in the language in good currency.

One would need to replace the reference to egalitarianism (a most confusing term that has come to connote an entitlement to equality of outcomes) by the more accurate, honest, and practical word *equability* — a term that *Merriam-Webster* defines as "lack of noticeable, unpleasant, or extreme variation or inequality." This word provides a more useful reference point in finding the right balance in the practical search for openness, inclusiveness, high performance, and the inescapable reality of differences. Equability does not entail uniformity.

SANITIZING THE LANGUAGE OF HUMAN RIGHTS

Human rights discourse is the new despotism. Do-gooders have been so intent on limiting the damages that the tyranny of a majority may inflict on minorities that they have come lyrically to defend the tyranny of minorities and have fallen into an idolatry of rights as if they were totems. As Michael Ignatieff rightly underlines, "We need to stop thinking of human rights as trumps and begin thinking of them as a language that creates a basis for deliberation" (2001, 95).

Rights are not a set of trump cards to bring political disputes to closure. Parliament is the place of last resort for deliberation about all governance issues in a democracy. The idea that Parliament is not to be trusted, and that judges as super-bureaucrats are like shamans who cannot be contested, is anti-democratic. The Charter of Rights and Freedoms is a creature of Parliament. Rights have been defined by Parliament. As Ignatieff says, they are a "tool kit against oppression," and one should not automatically "define anything desirable as a right," because that would then erode the legitimacy of core rights (2001, 57, 90).

Moreover, courts are not infallible in interpreting the charter. And there is nothing sinister, in a free and democratic society, in Parliament's use of the notwithstanding clause to suspend for a time the application of a decision by the courts that does not pertain to oppression and with which the majority of freely elected parliamentarians does not agree.

To allow minority groups to obtain everything that they *prefer* to have as a matter of right, to make rights into a secular religion and the courts into its only authorized clergy, will take us into dangerous territory. Unfortunately, this was exactly the discourse that seemed to be the gospel in good currency for the Martin government, and it was explicitly stated by its minister of justice, Irwin Cotler, in the *Ottawa Citizen* of June 16, 2004.

The second set of prerequisites has to do with developing a culture of risk taking and experimentation.

CONFRONTING OUR ORGANIZATIONAL CULTURE
The extent to which Canadian corporate culture has been individualist, inwardly directed, short-term oriented, and achievement focused has probably contributed significantly to a less than optimal investment in organizational capital and to a poorer organizational alignment of capabilities. The new mantra of the Canadian corporate scene (the "search for a culture of integrity" — that is, wholeness and completeness) compared with the mantra in the United States (a drive toward a "culture of confidence"; see www.chlglobalassociates.com) may be revealing: Canadian companies do not sense that they have been able to align their capabilities well enough to yield all the value adding that they know they can generate.

Too often dramatic/compulsive Canadian organizations have dealt only with surface adjustments (to look as though they are changing) and have done so in ways that have been so overcentralized that there has been no significant mobilization of the ebullience within them. There are many examples of how quickly a fruitful alignment of the capabilities of a Canadian organization can come unstuck and of how easily Canadian organizations can be drawn into wallowing in the safety of evasive thinking (e.g., vision and mission statements) instead of tackling more tangible commitments (e.g., partnerships).

One of the unintended consequences of the welfare state has been a de-responsibilization of the citizens as producers of governance. It has led to a culture of risk aversion. What has been forgotten in the process of reaping the benefits of the welfare state is that citizenship entails duties and responsibilities. This is the basis on which citizens are granted rights: to enable them to dispatch their responsibilities. Indeed, both negative and positive freedoms are guaranteed to the citizens for them to be able to perform their work as producers of governance.

But such guarantees entail first recognizing the limitations ascribable to our own corporate culture. Canada does not rank as high on individualism as the United States, the United Kingdom, or Australia. This lower ranking may be an echo effect of the welfare state era. Another major difference between Canada and the United States, mentioned earlier, is the dramatically greater degree of risk aversion in Canada. On this count, Canada closely resembles Latin American countries, where the degree of risk aversion is high.

BRICOLAGE, TRESPASSING, AND *MÉTISSAGE*

Corporate culture is at the core of "theory." Bricolage at the social technology level is likely to be much less threatening (and therefore not to be fought so fiercely) and so is more likely to lead less painfully to a change in both structure and theory. The central question is one of patience. In the history of the world, fifteen years (i.e., 5,000–6,000 days)—the time it might take to transform organizational culture—is rather a short period. For those, such as democratically elected politicians, however, who have a time horizon of three to four years, it may appear to be an eternity.

Bricolage is, indeed, a simple application of the process of tinkering that is at the core of what we have referred to earlier as prototyping and serious play.

Such thinking used to be at the core of Canadian culture—a sort of pragmatism that led Canada to invent a large number of contraptions to make the federation work in the pre-1972 period.

Innovative bricolage entails almost necessarily some trespassing and conversations across boundaries. Innovation is a social process, and the more successful the innovation, the more social the process. Lester and Piore (2004) describe the early stages of innovation as a cocktail party where diverse people gather and chat, casually but seriously, about a variety of topics in a safe and stimulating environment.

If one had to put a finger on the major failure of the Canadian institutional order, it might be the lack of such forums. Our overly rigid governing regime does not allow (or at least constrains) the free-form exchange of ideas, and this rigidity (together with the lack of forums) often condemns organizations to a future of "unimaginative product extensions" when what is needed is reframing. Emerson's lightbulb was not discovered on a search to improve the candle. Tinkering with information flows, creating new forums, and stimulating new partnerships may appear to be innocuous, but the sort of trespassing, bricolage, and *métissage* likely to ensue may hold the key to such reframing (Hubbard and Paquet 2006b).

CONCLUSION

It would not be prudent to predict a thawing of the Canadian ethos that will proceed in a revolutionary way or advance quickly. There may be a *perestroika* in the making, but it will proceed in a hesitant, meandering, two-steps-forward-and-one-step-back, and/or oblique fashion. This is the Canadian way.

Responses to the challenges of the new environment have begun to emerge from local communities, from entrepreneurs in social change, and from governments in need of regaining a sense of effectiveness and legitimacy. Although the new institutional order has not yet crystallized, the old order is showing signs of losing strength. Transformation is under way.

Our insistence on process at the end of this Gomery-inspired disquisition may appear to avoid dealing explicitly with the fabric of the new order. Had the Gomery inquiry led the charge on this front, the spirit of the citizenry might be ready for dramatic transformation. But by choosing to focus meekly on narrow financial accountability issues, Gomery planted the seed of discontent and generated some movement. Canadians are experimenting with a new government, and this is not unimportant. But one has to proceed carefully; it would take very little to make a risk-averse population run for cover.

Before experimenting too boldly, the citizenry of Canada must build the requisite "negative capacity" (as Keats would call it)—that is, the capacity to keep going when things are going wrong. Doing so entails construction of the necessary support systems to help the citizens both to take creative part in this multilogue and to withstand the chilling effect generated by the setbacks that will accompany any change venture of this sort.

Roy Lewis has analyzed this sort of situation in a satirical mode in his famous *What We Did to Father* (1960), in which he portrays the experience of a community of tree-dwelling apes discovering fire, inventing tools, and being carried forward by progress away from the security of their trees. In such a transitional world, every unfortunate event is always an occasion for reluctant participants to denounce progress and to launch a "back to the trees" movement.

Determination and resilience on such a road require more than a solid infrastructure; they can only be assured by some agreeing to become *savanturiers* (a crasis of *savant* and *aventurier*), as Raymond Queneau calls them. For those interested in such *savantures*, we intend to put forward some modest proposals in our forthcoming book, *Unfreezing the Canadian Ethos*. Whether it emerges sooner or later will depend not solely on our lack of fortitude or imagination but also on the Canadian societal context: our philosophy, like Paul Masson's, is never to serve a wine before its time.

NOTE

Although they have been modified and recombined a number of times, important segments of several chapters have been drawn from previously published papers.

"The $100-Million Mirage: A Cautionary Note," www.optimumonline. ca 34, 1 (2004): 3–7.

"Gomery as Glasnost," *Literary Review of Canada* 13, 7 (2005): 12–15.

"The Quail Enigma," www.optimumonline.ca 35, 3 (2005): 12–23.

« A propos de certains vices cachés du premier rapport Gomery, » *Ethique publique* 8, 1 (2006) : 160–165.

"Gomery II: Fear of Blurring and Lack of *Temperantia*," www. optimumonline.ca 36, 1 (2006): 7–22.

REFERENCES

Agamben, G. 2003. *État d'exception*. Paris: Seuil.

Alain. 1934. *Propos d'économique*. Paris: Gallimard.

Argyris, C., and D.A. Schön. 1974. *Theory in Practice*. San Francisco: Jossey-Bass.

Aubry, J. 2006. "Harper's Ethics Plan Falls Short: Watchdog." *Ottawa Citizen*, February 17.

Aucoin, P., and M. D. Jarvis. 2005. *Modernizing Government Accountability: A Framework for Reform*. Ottawa: Canada School of Public Service.

Bellah, R. N., et al. 1991. *The Good Society*. New York: Knopf.

Benoit, L. E., and C. E. S. Franks. 2006. "For the Want of a Nail: The Role of Internal Audit in the Sponsorship Scandal in Gomery II." *Research Studies* 2: 233–304.

Bliss, M. 2004. *Right Honourable Men: The Descent of Canadian Politics from Macdonald to Chrétien*. Toronto: HarperCollins.

Camus, A. 1956. *La chute*. Paris : Gallimard.

Chenier, J. A. 2004. "The Auditor General and Sponsorship: A Commentary." www.optimumonline.ca 34, no. 1: 2–3.

Clark, C. 2005. "Liberals Unveil New Bureaucratic Controls." *Globe and Mail*, October 26.

Clark, I., and H. Swain. 2005. "Distinguishing the Real from the Surreal in Management Reform: Suggestions for Beleaguered Administrators in the Government of Canada." *Canadian Public Administration* 48, no. 4: 453–76.

Cleveland, H. 2002. *Nobody in Charge*. San Francisco: Jossey-Bass.

Conservative Party of Canada (Federal Accountability Act). 2006. "Standing Up for Accountability." www.conservative.ca/media/20051104-Policy-Accountability3.pdf.

Cotler, I. 2004. "The Charter Is Here to Stay." *Ottawa Citizen,* June 16.

Crozier, M. 1987. *État modeste, état moderne.* Paris: Fayard.

Dörner, D. 1997. *The Logic of Failure.* Reading, MA: Addison-Wesley.

Duncan, G. 1985. "A Crisis of Social Democracy?" *Parliamentary Affairs* 38, no. 3: 267–81.

Etzioni, A. 1983. *An Immodest Agenda.* New York: McGraw-Hill.

Evans, P., and B. Wolf. 2005. "Collaboration Rules." *Harvard Business Review* 83, no. 7: 96-104.

Fisher, D. 2005. "Gomery Was a Whitewash." *Toronto Sun,* November 6.

Franks, C. E. S. 2004. "Putting Accountability and Responsibility Back into the System of Government." *Policy Options* 25, no. 9: 64–66.

Fukuyama, F. 2004. *State-Building.* Ithaca, NY: Cornell University Press.

Fuller, S. 2005. *The Intellectual.* Cambridge, U.K.: Icon Books.

Galston, W. A. 2002. *Liberal Pluralism.* Cambridge, U.K.: Cambridge University Press.

Goldsmith, S., and W. D. Eggers. 2004. *Governing by Network.* Washington, DC: Brookings Institution Press.

Gomery, J. H. 2004. Public hearing transcripts: November 3 (vol. 33), witness Joseph Charles Guité; November 24 (vol. 39) and November 25 (vol. 40), witness Ranald Quail; and November 29 (vol. 41), witness Richard Neville.

———. 2005. *Who Is Responsible?* Phase One Report of the Commission of Inquiry into the Sponsorship Program and Advertising Activities (Gomery I). Ottawa: Government of Canada.

———. 2006. *Restoring Accountability: Recommendations.* Phase Two Report of the Commission of Inquiry into the Sponsorship Program and Advertising Activities (Gomery II). Research Studies Volumes 1, 2, and 3. Ottawa: Government of Canada.

Government of Canada (GOC). 2003a. Guidance for Deputy Ministers, Privy Council Office. www.pco-bcp.gc.ca/default.asp?Page=Publications&Language=E&doc=gdm-gsm/gdm-gsm_doc_e.htm.

———. 2003b. Government Response to the Tenth Report of the Standing Committee on Public Accounts (last modified September 15). www.tbs-sct.gc.ca/report/gr-rg/grtr-rgdr_e.asp.

———. 2005. Government Response to the Tenth Report of the Standing Committee on Public Accounts, House of Commons, May 9. www.tbs-sct.gc.ca/gr-rg/2005/0817_e.asp.

Gow, J. I. 2004. *A Canadian Model of Public Administration?* Ottawa: Canada School of Public Service.

Habermas, J. 1973. *Legitimation Crisis.* Boston: Beacon.

Havel, V. 1991. *Open Letters.* London: Faber and Faber.

Hine, V. H. 1977. "The Basic Paradigm of a Future Socio-Cultural System." *World Issues* April-May: 19–22.

Hirsch, F. 1976. *Social Limits to Growth.* Cambridge, MA: Harvard University Press.

Hirschman, A. O. 1995. *A Propensity to Self-Subversion.* Cambridge, MA: Harvard University Press.

Hubbard, R. 2004. "Do We Need Super Bureaucrats?" www.optimumonline 34, no. 3: 38–43.

Hubbard, R., and G. Paquet. 2002. "Ecologies of Governance and Institutional *Métissage.*" www.optimumonline.ca 32, no. 4: 25–34.

———. 2005. "The Quail Enigma." www.optimumonline.ca 35, no. 3: 12–23.

———. 2006a. "Clerk as *Révélateur:* A Panoramic View." In P. Dutil, ed., *Leadership Lessons of Secretaries to Cabinet,* forthcoming. Toronto: Institute of Public Administration of Canada.

———. 2006b. "Réinventer notre architecture institutionnelle." *Options politiques* 27, no. 7 : 55–63.

Ibbitson, J. 2005. *The Polite Revolution.* Toronto: McClelland and Stewart.

Ignatieff, M. 2001. *Human Rights as Politics and Idolatry.* Princeton: Princeton University Press.

Jacobs, J. 1992. *Systems of Survival.* Toronto: Random House.

Kets de Vries, M. F. R., and D. Miller. 1984. *The Neurotic Organization.* San Francisco: Jossey-Bass.

Kettl, D. F. 2002. *The Transformation of Governance: Public Administration for Twenty-First Century America.* Baltimore: Johns Hopkins University Press.

King, A. 1975. "Overload: Problems of Governing in the Seventies." *Political Studies* 23, no. 2–3: 284–296.

Kroeger, A. 1996. "The Public Service in a Modern Democracy." Lecture to the Polish School of Public Administration, March 14.

———. 2006. "The Elected Should Have the Last Word." *Globe and Mail,* February 7.

Lachmann, L. M. 1971. *The Legacy of Max Weber.* Berkeley: Glendessary Press.

Le Grand, J. 2003. *Motivation, Agency, and Public Policy.* Oxford: Oxford University Press.

Leishman, R. 2006. *Against Judicial Activism.* Montreal: McGill-Queen's University Press.

Leiss, W. 2006. *Hera or Empathy.* Ottawa: Magnus and Associates.

Lesourne, J. 2003. *Ces avenirs qui n'ont pas eu lieu.* Paris : Odile Jacob.

Lester, R. K., and M. J. Piore. 2004. *Innovation: The Missing Dimension.* Cambridge, MA: Harvard University Press.

Lewis, R. 1960. *What We Did to Father.* London: Hutchinson.

Lowi, T. J. 1975. "Toward a Politics of Economics." In L. N. Lindberg et al., eds., *Stress and Contradiction in Modern Capitalism,* 115–24. Lexington: D. C. Heath.

Marquand, D. 1988. *The Unprincipled Society.* London: Fontana.

———. 2004. *Decline of the Public.* Cambridge, U.K.: Polity Press.

May, K. 2006a. "Report Is 'Foolish,' Says Expert Whose Work Was Cast Aside." *Ottawa Citizen,* February 28.

———. 2006b. "Canada's Elite to Harper: Don't Listen to This Man." *Ottawa Citizen,* February 27.

Mead, L. 1986. *Beyond Entitlement.* New York: Free Press.

Morgan, G. 1988. *Riding the Waves of Change.* San Francisco: Jossey-Bass.

O'Connor, J. 1973. *The Fiscal Crisis of the State.* New York: St. Martin's Press.

Office of the Auditor General. 2003. "The Sponsorship Program: Overall Main Points." In *Report of the Auditor General of Canada to the House of Commons: Government-Wide Audit of Sponsorship Program, Advertising, and Public Opinion Research,* Chapter 3. © Minister of Public Works and Government Services Canada (Tabled in Parliament February 2004.).

O'Neill, O. 2002. *A Question of Trust.* Cambridge, U.K.: Cambridge University Press.

Osbaldeston, G. 1988. "Dear Minister." *Policy Options* no. 9, 3: 4–11.

Paquet, G. 1992. "Betting on Moral Contracts." *Optimum* 22, no. 3: 45–53.

———. 1999a. *Governance through Social Learning.* Ottawa: University of Ottawa Press.

——. 1999b. "Innovations in Governance in Canada." www.optimumonline.ca 39, no. 2: 71–81.

——. 2004a. "The $100-Million Mirage: A Cautionary Note." www.optimumonline.ca 34, no. 1: 3–7.

——. 2004b. *Pathologies de gouvernance*. Montréal : Liber.

——. 2005a. "Gomery as *Glasnost*." *Literary Review of Canada* 13, no. 7: 12–15.

——. 2005b. "The RSC as Public Intellectual." www.optimumonline.ca 35, no. 4: 3–37.

——. 2005c. *Gouvernance: Une invitation à la subversion*. Montréal : Liber.

——. 2005d. *The New Geo-Governance: A Baroque Approach*. Ottawa: University of Ottawa Press.

——. 2005e. "Jean Charest's First 500 Days: Two Anamorphoses." *Policy Options* 26, no. 9: 73–75.

——. 2006a. « A propos de certains vices cachés du premier rapport Gomery. » *Ethique publique* 8, no. 1 : 160–65.

——. 2006b. "The Many Are Smarter than the Few" www.optimumonline.ca 36, no. 4: pp. 25–42 .

——. 2006c. « Une déprimante culture de l'adjudication. » *Policy Options* 27, no. 5 : 40–45.

Posner, R. A. 2003. *Law, Pragmatism, and Democracy*. Cambridge, MA: Harvard University Press.

Potter, A. 2006. "The Trouble with Gomery." *Maclean's*, February 20.

PWGSC. 2000. 2000-273. "Directed Audit of the Management of Sponsorship at the CCSB." www.pwgsc.gc.ca.

Reynolds, N. 2006. "Mr. Ignatieff's Mischievous Tax Argument." *Globe and Mail*, September 8.

Rittel, H. W. J., and M. M. Webber. 1973. "Dilemmas in a General Theory of Planning." *Policy Sciences* 4: 155–69.

Roberts, A. 2006. "Two Challenges in Administration of the Access to Information Act." In *Restoring Accountability: Recommendations, Research Studies* 2: 115–62.

Robertson, G. 2001 [2000]. *Memoirs of a Very Civil Servant*. Toronto: University of Toronto Press.

Saint-Onge, H., and C. Armstrong. 2004. *The Conductive Organization*. Amsterdam: Elsevier.

Savoie, D. J. 2003. *Breaking the Bargain*. Toronto: University of Toronto Press.

Schön, D. 1971. *Beyond the Stable State*. New York: Norton.

Schrage, M. 2000. *Serious Play*. Boston: Harvard Business School Press.

Sen, A. 1999. *Development as Freedom*. New York: Knopf.

Thacher, D., and M. Rein. 2004. "Managing Value Conflict in Public Policy." *Governance* 17, no. 4: 457–86.

The Economist. 2006. "The State Is Looking After You." April 18.

Treasury Board Secretariat. 1995a. *Framework for Alternative Program Delivery*. © Minister of Public Works and Government Services Canada.

———. 1995b. *Cadre d'examen des différents modes d'exécution des programmes*. © Ministre des Travaux publics et des Services gouvernementaux du Canada.

Vialatte, A. 1998. *Kafka ou l'innocence diabolique*. Paris: Les Belles Lettres.

Vickers, G. 1965. *The Art of Judgment*. London: Methuen.

Vonnegut, Jr., K. 1963. *Cat's Cradle*. New York: Delacorte Press.

Williams, J. 2005. "MPs Hold the Government's Feet to the Fire." *Ottawa Citizen*, August 24.

Wolfe, A. 1989. *Whose Keeper?* Berkeley: University of California Press.

INDEX